A Romance of the Turf

A Romance of the Turf

PARK TOP

The Duke of Devonshire

JOHN MURRAY
Albemarle Street, London

In Memory of B.v.C.

Acknowledgements

The photographs in this book appear with the permission of their originators, Messrs Wallis, Doncaster; Sport and General, London; and P. Bertrand et Fils, Paris.

The details of Park Top's racing career which comprise the appendix are reproduced by kind permission of their publishers, Raceform Ltd. and Raceform Up-to-Date, 55 Curzon Street, London W1.

First published by London Magazine Editions Ltd. 1976

Reissued in paperback in 2000
by John Murray (Publishers) Ltd.,
50 Albemarle Street, London W1X 4BD

A catalogue record for this book is available from the British Library

ISBN 0-7195-5482-9

Printed and bound in Great Britain by
The University Press, Cambridge

Contents

Illustrations appear between pages 64 and 65

Foreword

Anyone who needs to be told that racehorse ownership represents the purest form of economic suicide has never received a training account. Yet in any given year, in Great Britain alone, more than 10,000 citizens are responsible as proprietors for the support of one of nature's greater glories, the thoroughbred racehorse.

There are many difficulties associated with horseracing, not the least of which is the commonly shared problem of separating bookmakers from their money. Another even greater conundrum is how to convey to uncommitted 'suicides' the depth of emotion evoked by invariably elusive success.

That the author of *A Romance of the Turf* achieves this delicate feat while relating – in pure, unpretentious prose – the story of his great mare is incidental to the narrative; but it is the ingredient of this delightful book that makes it a classic of its genre. As journalist and broadcaster I was privileged to witness both the romantic career of the bargain-basement achiever of her era and, importantly, the marvellous team who guided her destiny. Among abiding memories for this aficionado is the afternoon of 26 July 1969 when, in the King George VI and Queen Elizabeth Stakes, barely prompted by the incomparable Lester Piggott, the now five-year-old mare gave a brilliant impersonation of Pegasus as she 'took off' in the short Ascot straight and, exchanging last place for first in an eyeblink, floated past eight rivals to achieve the tenth of her thirteen victories.

Then there was the contrasting occasion at Longchamp on Sunday, 11 October 1970, when she started 100–30 on in the seven-runner Prix de Royallieu. My 'copy' on the following day was captioned, 'Lester Piggott is jeered as Park Top flops'. The record-breaking mare had been ridden well off the pace as usual but, unsuited to the rain-softened ground and lacking the sparkle of youth, she simply could not produce the old magic.

It was sad enough to see her trailing former inferiors – dead-heating for third place, three and a half lengths behind the winner – without the Gallic *turfistes'* disreputable demonstration which John Oaksey wrote of as 'a bestial scene'. Small wonder that the Duke of Devonshire, by way of defending his jockey, faced the jeering paddockside mob and forcefully raised his two fingers in what I referred to in my report as 'a clearly less-than-Ducal gesture'.

In short, this beguiling book is the story of a star, written by another.

Peter O'Sullevan

7

Author's Note

While the heroine of this book is Park Top it also has a hero, Bernard van Cutsem, whose discerning eye picked her out and bought her as a yearling and whose skill as a trainer made her a great race-horse.

I first met Bernard in the summer of 1938, suitably enough while racing at Sandown. My elder brother, Billy, had become a friend of his while they were at Cambridge together. When I went up that autumn he was training a few steeplechasers at Exning, near Newmarket and he used to drive several of us to the race-courses round London. By the time the war came we were firm friends. We continued to see something of each other, at one time both serving in units of the Guards Armoured Division while it was stationed in England. After the war, Bernard bought Northmore House and Stud at Exning, but did not re-apply for a trainer's licence, concentrating on farming and building up his stud. I was lucky enough to become a regular guest for the Spring, Summer and Autumn Meetings at Newmarket.

Through the indulgence of my father, I bought my first race-horse in 1948 and as Bernard was not training I sent it to Marcus Marsh. Bernard took out a licence in 1957 and I sent him my horses when Marcus retired in 1963; it was one of the most sensible things I have ever done.

While in the eighteen years he was training Bernard was to prove himself a master of his craft, in his early days he had his critics. With his Belgian name and El Greco-like face many in the highly prejudiced world of racing were suspicious of him.

8

He was known to like a gamble and the uninformed regarded him at a "hot" trainer who might run his horses when they were not trying so that on the chosen day, having been duly backed, they would win at a long price. Nothing was farther from the truth; in racing, as in everything else, Bernard was the most honourable of men. His right-wing views, vividly expressed over the dinner table, antagonised some people, yet those who worked for him loved him and were intensely loyal to him. Frank Morby, now riding with such success, worked at Stanley House Stables for twelve years and is on record as describing Bernard as "the perfect Governor". During the 1975 stable-lads strike, out of a work force of about forty only one from his yard joined the strikers and that one, I believe, only on the insistence of his wife.

As a man, Bernard's outstanding qualities were generosity and loyalty, to which he added beautiful manners. During his illness in 1969, and its tragic re-occurrence which led to his death in December 1975, he showed courage and fortitude which had to be witnessed to be believed. As a trainer he was totally dedicated to his work, he would allow nothing to come before his job of training race-horses. Although he loved grouse shooting and was a brilliant shot, in vain would I ask him to stay for two or three days in August; once he did accept for one day, only to leave at lunchtime to watch one of the least distinguished horses in his charge run at nearby Pontefract races. This was typical of him. He took endless trouble to place moderate or even downright bad horses in races which they could win. Apart from the genius he showed in training Park Top for five years, his handling of such horses as High Top, Decies, Karabas, Mountain Call, Noble Decree, Crowned Prince, Sharpen Up and a host of others is proof to his ability to train top-class horses of all ages over all distances. As he grew older, his enthusiasm for betting in substantial sums waned but he was characteristically open-handed in letting his friends know when he fancied a horse and on these occasions it was rarely far away at the finish.

As the years went by, more and more owners wished him to take their horses, including some who in his early days had been chief among his critics. By the end of the 1960s Stanley House Stables were full to overflowing and Bernard found himself having to turn patrons away.

Owning Park Top has been one of the great experiences of my life. The pleasure and happiness it has given me were greatly enhanced by the fact that she was trained by Bernard. For this, and for the thirty-seven years of his friendship, I shall be forever grateful.

A.D.

1967
From the Mar Lodge to
the Ribblesdale

This is the story of Park Top, a bay thorougbred mare by Kalydon out of Nellie Park. She was foaled on May 27th 1964, her owner and breeder was Mrs. Scott, of the Buttermilk Stud, Banbury.

I was not to know of her existence until she came up for sale nearly eighteen months later at Tattersalls on the morning of October 14th 1965. This is more surprising than it sounds, since I had bought and owned Nellie Park throughout her brief racing career. It is perhaps of interest to know why I bought her, and why later Mrs. Scott in turn acquired her from me as a brood mare. Nellie Park was by Arctic Prince out of Oola Hills. Although Arctic Prince won the Derby in 1951 by ten lengths, he was not an outstanding Derby winner. He only ran five times, winning a small race at Redcar as a two-year-old from two starts. As a three-year-old, he was unplaced in the Two Thousand Guineas before winning the Derby. It was in her dam, Oola Hills, that Nellie Park's attraction lay, both for me when buying her as a yearling and for Mrs. Scott when she bought her six years later for 480 guineas. Oola Hills was the dam of Pappa Fourway, one of the fastest horses seen on the English turf since the war. He won twelve races in all, four as a two-year-old, and was unbeaten in all his eight starts as a three-year-old. Among his victories were the King's Stand Stakes at Royal Ascot, the July Cup at Newmarket, and the Diadem

Stakes at Ascot Heath. Nellie Park was therefore a half-sister, by a Derby winner, to a truly great five- and six-furlong horse, with her blood lines combining speed and stamina.

I bought Nellie Park for a dual purpose. I hoped she would be a good race mare and would then be a valuable addition to the small stud I was building up at Newmarket. In the event things turned out differently. Nellie Park went to be trained by Marcus Marsh at Newmarket, who had been in charge of my horses since I first became an owner in 1949. Up till 1956, the year I bought Nellie Park, and indeed until the advent of Park Top's racing career in 1967, I had not been a lucky owner. Over the years I had owned a considerable number of horses, but they had been without exception very moderate animals. Such few races as I had won were of little account. Nellie Park was no exception. As a two-year-old she did not run, which is only of interest when the exploits of her famous daughter are considered. At three, she ran five times without winning. She was however second twice, and third once, in modest races for horses which had not previously won. The distance of these races varied from one mile to a mile and a half. Thus it was clear that she had none of the brilliant speed of her half-brother Pappa Fourway, and such little ability as she did have came from the stamina of her Derby-winning sire. Nellie Park was then retired to stud and in due course sent to the French-bred stallion Tropique. She was in foal to him when I sent her up to the December sales of 1961 where she became the property of Mrs. Scott.

Looking back I do not know why, having bought Nellie Park partly as a prospective mare, I sold her before she had had a chance to prove herself at stud. At the time I was a Junior Minister at the Commonwealth Relations Office and had little time for racing. I can only presume that owing to the combination of her lack of success and my lack of time to think about racing and breeding, I decided that the easiest way of settling the mare's future was to sell her. Her sale was the first of the many twists of fortune that were to mark Park Top's history. Had I kept her there is no reason to suppose I would have sent her to the same sire as Mrs. Scott chose.

To turn now to Park Top's sire, Kalydon. He was owned and bred by Bernard van Cutsem, who was later to buy and train Park Top for me. Kalydon was an extremely well-bred horse, being by the Gold Cup winner Alycidon, who represented the best of the famous Stanley House Stud blood, out of Lackaday, a good race mare with a pedigree tracing to a family that has proved to be a prolific producer of winners. Kalydon ran twice, unplaced, as a two-year-old. At three he proved himself to be a top-class staying colt, winning among other races the Commonwealth Stakes over a mile and five furlongs at Sandown, and the Oxfordshire Stakes over the same distance at Newbury, by three lengths and six lengths respectively. He started second-favourite for the St. Leger, but was unplaced.

Nellie Park's foal by Tropique, which she was carrying when Mrs. Scott bought her, proved to be of no account. The mare was then sent to Matador, a sprinting sire, but unfortunately she slipped the foal. In 1963 came the momentous decision to send Nellie Park to Kalydon.

Mrs. Scott's reasons for doing this were, in her own words : "I had always admired this beautifully-bred horse, Kalydon, and felt sure that he would sire a top class horse if given the chance. In spite of a considerable amount of staying blood in her pedigree, I considered the very fast blood in Nellie Park's dam, Oola Hills, would offset this and that it should produce a very good middle-distance horse." The result was Park Top.

What, looking back, was the strangest part was that although she was bought at public auction, her sire was owned by her trainer and her dam had once been the property of her new

The property of Buttermilk Stud—continued.

At Park Paddocks, Somerville Paddock, Boxes 162 to 164.

180

A BAY FILLY
(second living foal),
Foaled
May 27th, 1964

	Kalydon	Alycidon	Donatello II
			Aurora
		Lackaday	Bobsleigh
			Lackadaisy
	Nellie Park (1957)	Arctic Prince	Prince Chevalier
			Arctic Sun
		Oola Hills	Denturius
			Chikoo

NELLIE PARK was placed second twice and third once, from five starts, at 3 years, her only season to race; her three-year-old colt, Gaffer, has been placed, this year; her first foal and only runner to date.

OOLA HILLS did not race; dam of **Ragwell** (winner and placed second in Ireland), **Pappa Fourway** (won 12 races, £9889, including July Cup, King's Stand Stakes, Ascot, Diadem Stakes, Gosforth Park, Festival Stakes, and Moulton Stakes, unbeaten winner of eight races at 3 years, and successful sire in U.S.A.), **Wilton Road** (winner at 2 years), **Wasps Fifteen** (won two races, £744, including Sussex Handicap Stakes, Brighton, and placed second in Cork and Orrery Stakes, and third in Queen Elizabeth Handicap Stakes, Kempton Park, also dam of a winner), Nellie Park, and Ruidoso (placed second at 2 years in 1961).

CHIKOO only raced at 2 years, twice; dam of Pappachik (winner over hurdles and placed three times under N.H. Rules), Oola Hills, and Princess Koo (placed second in Ireland), from only nine foals. The next dam, Chor Bazar, won, and dam of Fekri, winner, and is half-sister to eight winners, including Theft (won £10,618), Bala Hissar (won Dewhurst Stakes), and Le Voleur (won £4085). Her dam, Voleuse, is by Volta, out of Sun Worship (dam of Solario, won St. Leger, Ascot Gold Cup, and £20,935, also grandam of Museum, won Irish Derby, St. Leger, and 2000gs., also Phideas, winner of Irish Derby and 2000gs.), by Sundridge.

owner. Park Top was actually foaled at the Tudor Stud and returned in the summer to Buttermilk with her dam. As a foal and yearling she was always easy to handle with a very placid temperament and she never caused any trouble.

As a yearling, she developed into a beautiful filly of medium size. As Mrs. Scott had no other filly for her to run with, her companions were Mrs. Scott's own old pony Blossom, and some cattle. The two horses became inseparable companions. Only once did the yearling give her breeder an indication of things to come. The filly was galloping along a stretch of grass at the bottom of her paddock when Mrs. Scott saw her produce an electrifying burst of speed, so remarkable that Mrs. Scott could only describe it to her husband as "quite extraordinary". In the years to come, that "quite extraordinary" burst of speed was to become famous on the race-courses of England and France as the hallmark of Park Top's greatness.

Before going into the auction ring at Tattersalls on the morning of October 14th 1965, Bernard had been the only person to visit Nellie Park's yearling filly. It is reasonable to suppose that he did this because he owned the sire; whatever the reason he was well pleased with what he saw. At about 10.30 a.m. she was knocked down for 500 guineas, the all too modest reserve placed on her by Mrs. Scott, to John Hislop, bidding on Bernard's behalf.

I was to hear of the purchase later that day. I had asked Bernard, who trained my horses at Stanley House, Newmarket, to buy me two yearlings at the Sales and in due course he rang up to say he had bought me a yearling filly. He told me he liked her very much but was worried by the price she had fetched. Fearing that this meant the yearling had cost a great deal of money I asked nervously how much he had had to pay. To my relief, the answer was that the filly had cost 500 guineas. I then asked who the filly was by. Again Bernard was apologetic, replying that she was by his own stallion Kalydon, who up till then had not been an outstanding success as a sire. Finally, I asked the name of the dam, and when told Nellie Park I replied, possibly a little sharply, that she was pretty useless as I knew to my cost since I had owned her. This was news to Bernard, but there was no reason why he should have known as she had not been trained by him. I had only sent my horses to him when Marcus Marsh had retired in 1963. However, I told Bernard I was delighted to have the filly and, at that price, it would not matter much if she turned out to be a disappointment.

It was not until many months later that Bernard told me the

15

true story of how I came to be Park Top's owner. I had been only one of a number of people who had asked him to buy them yearlings. Amongst them had been a vastly rich American coming in to racing for the first time. It had been Bernard's original intention to pass on the Nellie Park filly to him. On second thoughts, he had got cold feet at buying such a cheap yearling for a multi-millionaire who had told him that when buying money was no object. Bernard, knowing I would have no objection, indeed the reverse, to paying a low price, decided to offer her to me instead. Such was the first of my two great strokes of luck in owning Park Top.

The next thing to do was to name her. Finding good names for race-horses is one of the minor joys of ownership. Ideally the name should combine something of the names of both the horse's sire and dam. A perfect example was the late Lord Stanley's great staying mare Quashed who was by Obliterate out of Verdict. However, owing to the large number of horses in training it is increasingly difficult to get the names one wants, and I had taken to calling my horses after the names of the various drives on my family's grouse moor in Yorkshire. Nellie Park was one such name. I quickly decided to call her daughter Park Top as it brought in the word Park and is also the name of the ground where, by tradition, we start the grouse shooting season on August 12th. It is in itself an uninspiring name but it is a good example of how names acquire a magic of their own from their association with the achievements of a great horse. Arkle, Brown Jack and Mill Reef are other examples that immediately come to mind.

Park Top took up her new quarters at Stanley House, under the expert eye of its master. It was clear from her earliest days that Bernard had a high regard for the filly since he put her in the hands of Maureen Foley. Quite apart from being a charming and delightful lady, Maureen has an immense talent for looking

16

after horses, particularly fillies and mares. It is impossible to over-estimate the importance to a thoroughbred's racing career of the part played by the lad or girl who looks after it. He or she is the human being with whom the horse is in constant contact. The lad or, as in this case, the girl not only grooms the horse twice a day, she also feeds and rides the horse at exercise daily. Maureen's loving attention played a vital part in Park Top's progress. She devoted endless hours to the horse throughout the four years Park Top resided at Stanley House. Maureen loved and cosseted her, even to the extent of post-poning her own wedding day to fit in with the mare's racing programme.

On her arrival at Stanley House, Park Top, like all the other newly arrived yearlings, went through the usual processes of being broken, first being lunged, then backed, then ridden away, until finally she was sufficiently advanced to canter in single file with the others round the home paddocks.

On January 1st 1966, Park Top became a two-year-old, since all thoroughbreds foaled in Europe and North America are auto-matically given the age of two on the 1st of January of the second year after that of their birth. Since she was a late foal, being born at the end of May 1965, Park Top was only a little more than eighteen months old on the first of January. Partly due to this, she was a backward two-year-old. In any case this was to be expected as her sire had run twice as a two-year-old and had not shown any of his true ability until he was three, while her dam had not raced at all as a two-year-old. One of Bernard's many skills as a trainer was his willingness to show endless patience with his horses. He allowed them to grow and develop their full potential before asking them to get down to the business of galloping at racing pace. There is no doubt that this patient attitude paid handsome dividends with Park Top.

In her two-year-old days she presented a more serious training problem than mere backwardness since she did not have the best of forelegs. Her fetlock joints were rather round, usually regarded as a sign of weakness. These doubtful joints gave Bernard further reason not to hurry Park Top's training programme. In the late spring the filly went lame. X-rays revealed that she had a small piece of loose bone in her near hock. This required an operation which in turn resulted in her training programme being put back several weeks It was not until the second half of the season that she began to do any serious work (the training expression for galloping at morning exercise rather than just cantering). However, as soon as Bernard asked her to gallop in earnest Park Top developed a cough. This put paid to any idea of giving her a race before the end of the season.

The cough, or equine influenza, is one of the greatest bugbears of a race-horse trainer's life. The symptoms are a cough and a running nose, accompanied by a temperature; as in human influenza, there are many variations of the illness and many degrees of its seriousness. Having the cough may result in the horse being laid off exercise for anything from a few days to a matter of months. In recent years, veterinary science has devised injections against the complaint. These have not proved to be a hundred per cent effective and the virus continues to bedevil trainers' lives.

In Park Top's case, getting the cough when she was a two-year-old was probably a blessing in disguise. For having once had it she was never a victim again. She may well have become immune to it in the same way as human beings only catch measles or chicken-pox once in their lives. This immunity was to prove invaluable. Three years later in 1969, the year of her greatest triumphs, there was a particularly virulent epidemic of coughing that nearly brought racing to a standstill in this country. Bernard's stable, like virtually every other training establishment, was badly hit. Park Top was almost the only horse in his yard that remained unaffected.

So the racing season of 1966 came and went without Park Top appearing on the race-course. It had been a poor year for me, as had the previous one. The number of winners I had had since my horses had been trained by Bernard could be counted on the fingers of one hand. I had brought nothing but bad luck to my previous trainer Marcus Marsh, and I was beginning to feel that having me in the yard was something of the kiss of death for the unfortunate trainer.

Not surprisingly, I did not view the start of the 1967 flat racing season with any great expectations. When the season opened Park Top had got over her troubles of the previous year. The effects of the cough had been shaken off and with patience and care her forelegs had improved.

Her first appearance on a race-course was delayed until the end of May. The future was to show she never came to her best until the warm weather arrived and she had had some sun on her back. The chosen day was May 22nd, just five days before her third birthday. The race was the Mar Lodge Plate at Windsor over a mile and a quarter and worth £345 to the winner. It was confined to three-year-old maidens, that is horses who have never won a race. It was evening racing, and the last race on the card. I drove down to Windsor, hopeful but far from confident. I had had too many disappointments over the years to be anything other than wary of the chances of any horse of mine winning. In any event, being confident of winning a race beforehand is asking for trouble. Bernard van Cutsem fancied the filly's chance and persuaded me to have my maximum bet. Having backed her, I joined him and Peggy Petre on the stand. Bernard asked me what price I had got and when I told him six to one he could hardly believe I had got such marvellous odds. This encouraged me to return to the rails and double my bet. In the end she started second favourite at five to one. This was to be the longest price she was ever to start at in a race in England.

By choosing a race of a mile and a quarter for Park Top's first appearance Bernard showed he was satisfied that Kalydon had passed on his stamina to the filly. That she would stay was to be expected since what little ability Nellie Park had shown had also been over a distance of ground.

There were fourteen runners of which only two had been placed in a previous race. Three others were, like Park Top, having their first outing. The favourite was Court Gem, trained by K. Cundell, who was to finish third and, like the second, Lord Sing, was to win a small race later in the season. Park Top gave her jockey Russ Maddock no trouble at the start, and the field was soon on its way. Windsor is a figure of eight course, and for races over a mile and a quarter the horses set off going away from the stands. Russ settled Park Top near the rear of the field where she remained for the first three-quarters of a mile of the twisting and turning track. Four furlongs out, she moved closer to the leaders and entering the straight just over two furlongs from home Russ's straw-coloured jacket could be seen close to the leaders.

Now in the early dusk, with the mist beginning to rise from the Thames, my pale yellow silks gleamed as Russ took Park Top to the front rather more than a furlong out and brought her home an easy winner by a length and a half. She won without being seriously pressed and there had been no question of Russ going for his whip.

The instant when victory is assured, and in particular the split second when your colours flash first past the post suddenly, make the whole business of racing worth while. All past disappointments are forgotten, the world is transformed into an entirely different place. Walking on air I accompanied Bernard to the unsaddling ring to await the filly's return. This moment in the winner's enclosure is another of the great thrills of racing. The full realisation of success has had time to sink in, and all the tension has gone. In due course, a smiling Russ Maddock rode Park Top into her place of privilege, to be greeted by Bernard, Maureen and myself, all equally delighted. There was laughter and mutual congratulations all round. Then when she had been led away to the race-course stables, and Russ had passed the scales, Bernard and I sought the nearest bar to celebrate and discuss future plans.

A successful race-horse's career, particularly in its early stages, is a series of tests each more severe than the last. Park Top had passed her first test with flying colours. She had shown that she was good enough to win a modest maiden race and her next would provide a stiffer task. In the bar Bernard suggested that provided she showed no ill effects as a result of the race, Park Top should next run in the Twyford Stakes at Newbury on June 14th, just over three weeks ahead. The distance would again be a mile and a quarter and although the race was for three-year-old fillies only, it was not confined to maidens. Park Top was therefore likely to meet horses who had already won. The race would be a step up in class and give a further indication of her ability. Bernard now also told me, for the first time, of his hopes to run Park Top in the mile and a half Ribblesdale Stakes at Ascot in the week following the Twyford Stakes. If she was good enough to win at Newbury, then he wanted her to take her chance against some of the best of her age and sex at the Royal Meeting.

I went back to London a happy man. Not only had I won a race, but equally if not even more exciting was the prospect of having a runner at Royal Ascot where, in the eighteen years I had owned horses, I had yet to see my colours carried.

One of the joys of winning a race is to read about it in the sporting pages of the newspapers the following morning. In this case however, it had to be a pleasure deferred. The result of the last race at an evening meeting at Windsor did not cause any comment. Most of the racing journalists had, in any case, gone home before it even took place. However I was happy enough with the summary of the race in *The Sporting Life*.

Park Top's win had not gone entirely unnoticed. One of the leading racing correspondents, the late and deeply mourned Clive Graham, famous as The Scout of the *Daily Express*, was to make a most remarkable prophecy on the morning of the Twyford Stakes when he made Park Top his Nap selection. This is what he wrote: "It's Park Top to land the Nap. Windsor is not generally considered the most likely place to introduce a top-class three-year-old, but Bernard van Cutsem produced a useful filly in Park Top at the last meeting there. Park Top, who had plenty in hand when carrying the Duke of Devonshire's colours to victory, could confirm her claim to a much greater future by taking Newbury's Twyford Stakes this evening."

Park Top was none the worse for her successful visit to Windsor. She continued to thrive and to please Bernard in her work. The Newbury race had much in common with the one at Windsor; the distance was the same, it was the last race of an evening meeting, and Park Top started second favourite.

The fillies she had to beat, however, were of a higher calibre than the opposition at Windsor. The most dangerous of them appeared to be Kathy III, owned by Lady Sassoon and trained by Noel Murless. On her first appearance of the season she had easily beaten a large field of maiden fillies over a mile and a quarter at Sandown. Third in that race had been another filly of mine, Anna Boleyna; at home Bernard considered this filly and Park Top much of a muchness with, if anything, Anna

Boleyna slightly the better. At Sandown, Kathy III had finished five and a half lengths ahead of my filly, so clearly Park Top had a battle ahead of her. Also among the field of five was the Queen's reputedly useful filly Caramel, by Crepello, who in her previous race had been third in a good class race at Newmarket.

The Twyford Stakes was worth £409 to the winner, and if Park Top was to have any chance at Ascot the following week she had to win, and win easily. Russ again rode her, and again he settled her down at the back of the small field. There she remained until half-way up the home straight. Then with two furlongs to run Park Top showed, for the first time on a race-course, that electrifying burst of speed that two years earlier had so astonished Mrs. Scott. When Russ gave Park Top her head she went from last to first in a matter of a few strides. Indeed, the race commentator had no sooner announced that Park Top was lying last than with the next breath he was saying Park Top had struck the front. At the post she had four lengths to spare over Caramel, with Russ sitting up against her and her ears pricked.

My wife Debo, who had missed the Windsor race, was with me and we could hardly believe our eyes as the filly showed her true brilliance for the first time. At Windsor she had gradually pulled her way to the front and there had been no need for her to produce her great turn of foot. Now we knew, or at least we had a pretty good idea, that in Park Top we had a top class filly who had inherited her sire's stamina and, more important, had the speed that her grand dam Oola Hills had imparted to the great sprinter Pappa Fourway, Park Top's equine uncle. All doubts about running her in the Ribblesdale were set aside and Russ for one was confident she would win it.

* * *

Owning race-horses is usually regarded as the pastime of the idle rich, although two Prime Ministers this century, Sir Winston Churchill and the 4th Earl of Rosebery, were prominent owners in their day. There will always be many who can see no point in racing, whose blood will never be stirred by the excitement and colour of the race-course. Both my mother and father hated racing. I once asked my mother why she disliked it so and she replied that whenever she had gone racing, she found herself walking in the opposite direction to everybody else, while my uncle Bobbity Salisbury, when he found himself at the Derby the year Sir Ivor won, was asked if he had seen Sir Ivor, to which he replied "Sir Ivor who?" Certainly racing devotees have only themselves to blame if they give racing a bad image. Their endless racing shop is as boring a topic of conversation as can be imagined. They are like Cole Porter's Mrs. Lousbrough-Goodby, whose friends talked racing, racing, and racing. When gathered together we seem to assume an arrogant air, as much as to say that racing is not only the sport of kings but that those who indulge in it are superior mortals, while those who do not are to be pitied and looked down upon.

Nevertheless for countless thousands of people racing has a peculiar fascination, of which betting is only one aspect. This fascination is difficult to analyse; obviously, beauty is a strong element, for thoroughbreds are noble, handsome animals, and the gaudy silks worn by the jockeys enhance their beauty. Then, there is the noise of horses galloping : there is no more thrilling sound than the collective thunder of horses' hooves as they race for the winning post. To all this must be added the excitement of the race itself, with all its hopes and expectations, hopes which are triumphantly fulfilled or cruelly exposed as vain aspirations within the twinkling of an eye.

There may be some philistines among those who follow racing, but there are many who are not. Race-horses and racing have attracted painters of the highest calibre ever since the sport first took roots in this country at the end of the seventeenth century. Among the first was the Dutchman Tillemans, who painted scenes of Newmarket Heath in the early part of the eighteenth century – a scene in which today only the garb of the riders and grooms have changed. After Tillemans came a host of others including John Wootton and James Seymour, both of whom painted Flying Childers owned by my ancestor the 2nd Duke of Devonshire. This horse was reputed to be "the fleetest horse that ever ran at Newmarket, or as is generally believed, that was ever bred in the world". Next there was Stubbs, although he only painted one picture of an actual race in progress, and that is in the background. This is his famous picture of Eclipse at the Rubbing House at Newmarket. Not long afterwards came Francis Sartorius, Ben Marshall, John Ferneley and John Francis Herring, and after him his son, also John Francis. The Impressionists had their admirers of the racing scene in Degas, Monet and Toulouse-Lautrec, while in more conventional style there were Emil Adam and Lynwood Palmer, and in more recent times Alfred Munnings.

The great nineteenth-century novelists were also aware of the fascination of racing. It comes into Disraeli's novels and plays an important part in the fifth of Trollope's great political series, *The Dukes' Children*, while his *The Kellys and the O'Kellys* has the winning of the Derby as one of the main strands in the plot. More recently, Galsworthy brought in many knowledgeable references to racing in his books, and the grandstand at Epsom holds the centre of the background of the view from The Hollies, old Jolyon's house in the Forsyte Saga. On a humbler level there have been many racing novelists from Nat Gould and Edgar Wallace to Dick Francis.

Racing has its place in the arts because of its beauty, glamour and drama. For owners, breeders and trainers it has a further great attraction, for it is a sport in which it is extremely difficult to be successful. For owners and breeders there can be no sure way to success. Certainly, anyone with the money can buy their way into racing, but they cannot be sure they are buying success. Many is the man who has spent a king's ransom on yearlings only to be rewarded with scant success. Luck is an essential element. One leading French trainer is reputed to enquire if approached by an owner to take his horses, not whether the man can be relied upon to pay his training bills or whether he is easy to get on with and to work for, but "is he lucky?" Only those who are involved in racing know just how difficult it is to win a race of even the most modest kind. For those who love racing it is the extreme competitiveness of the sport which makes winning a race, any race, the most exciting thing in the world.

Until recently the Ribblesdale was, by tradition, the last race of the second day at Royal Ascot. It is for three-year-old fillies over the classic distance of a mile and a half. In 1967 I was a Steward of the Jockey Club and the Senior Steward had convened a meeting on the course for 11.30 that morning. Thus I arrived with six hours to wait before Park Top had to face her great challenge. It was to be the moment of truth, when we were to know whether she really was a top class animal as she had led us to hope, or just another decent staying three-year-old filly.

The hours dragged by. Debo was in Scotland with her Shetland ponies at the Highland Show, so I was on my own. It was tempting just to retire to the bar and drink the hours and the tension away. After a seeming eternity the clock showed 4.45 and I went up to the far end of the paddock, just outside the race-course proper on the edge of the car park, to the preliminary parade ring. Here I found Park Top with the ever faithful Maureen walking her round. As usual they were both beautifully turned out and looking totally unperturbed. I leant over the rail and watched them. Shortly afterwards I was joined by Bernard; neither of us spoke as he too felt the tension, for he knew how much winning would mean to me. He was equally under the spell of the filly, a spell she cast over all those who came in contact with her. There was something quite special about her, everyone at Stanley House felt it. Watching her walk round you could sense her high intelligence, her interest in everything that was going on around her. She had a great presence, showing herself magnificently, and she reacted to the admiration of the crowd. This admiration visibly stimulated her, another aspect of her star quality.

The minutes dragged by but eventually it was time for her to be saddled and then to appear in the main parade ring. There was a field of twelve of which one was outstanding, St. Pauli Girl by the Derby winner St. Paddy, owned by Stanhope Joel and trained by Humphrey Cottrill. A fortnight before she had been a close second to Pia in the Oaks. There was thus no doubt of there being a truly classic filly in the field to test Park Top. The other runners included Plotina, by Hugh Lupus and trained by Noel Murless, who had won three of her six races as a two-year-old; and a useful filly of Jakie Astor's called The Nun who had won her last race, the Lancashire Oaks, also over a mile and a half. There were also a number of other good-looking fillies in the field as was to be expected in a race of this class.

Owing to her comparatively humble origins and to being backward, Park Top had not been entered for the Oaks. In any case she would not have been ready to run in it. She had only had her first race just over a fortnight before the Epsom classic was run and she would not have been forward enough to do herself justice. Now, however, with the experience of two races behind her, Bernard was prepared to let her take on all-comers.

As at Windsor and Newbury she was second favourite, this time at nine to two, with St. Pauli Girl the six-to-four favourite and Plotina the best backed of the others at eleven to two.

Park Top looked magnificent parading in front of the stands before the race and equally impressive cantering back to the start. As usual she gave no trouble entering the stalls. Lester Piggott was to say of her later that she entered the stalls like an old lady going to church and came out of them like a bat out of hell.

A horse called Silk II, ridden by Scobie Breasley made the early running as the horses flowed down to Swinley Bottom. Russ had Park Top just behind the leading bunch as they went past the mile gate and swung gradually right-handed up the hill. With six furlongs left Silk II and Shamrock Beauty were in the lead. The Ascot straight is comparatively short, just over two furlongs, and it is usually regarded as essential to be well placed at the final bend to hold a winning chance. Approaching the turn Shamrock Beauty still led from Silk II with St. Pauli Girl third, Plotina fourth, and Park Top fifth just ahead of The Nun. Before making the turn Russ switched the filly to the outside to get a clear run which cost him a little ground. Watching from the stands I thought she was fading and her chance gone.

I need not have worried. Park Top was full of running as the bell sounded, denoting that the field was rounding the turn into the straight. Once in line for home St. Pauli Girl struck the front, with Plotina second. Russ decided it was time to go. In a flash he had overtaken Shamrock Beauty and Plotina; and the next few strides settled the issue. Park Top shot past St. Pauli Girl and into the lead. There was still a furlong to run but though St. Pauli Girl ran on with great gameness she could make no impression. At the post Park Top held the advantage by half a length.

Such a winning margin sounds like a close finish, but once she had taken the lead Park Top was never in danger of defeat. As she went past the post she had her ears pricked and Russ was sitting still. It was an unforgettable sight, St. Pauli Girl carrying Stanhope Joel's green and pink stripes contrasting with Park Top's pale yellow. If at Windsor and Newbury the straw colours had shone out in the gloaming, here at Ascot they glittered and sparkled under the June sun. Their brilliance seemed to epitomise all the glory and panache of Royal Ascot on a perfect summer's afternoon.

Although it was the last race, the winner's unsaddling enclosure was packed, the crowd seemed to have sensed that a new star had arrived. It was like the triumphant performance of a little-known actress in a West End first night. Maureen, though wreathed in smiles, was as cool and calm as ever and Bernard too was never one to show his feelings. It is, though, one of racing's peculiarities that one is closer to tears in victory than in defeat; and this occasion for me was no exception.

Afterwards we gathered up all the friends we could find and went and sat on the terrace at the back of the bar behind the stand. There followed moments of pure, golden happiness as the shadows of the ilex trees that surround the terrace lengthened in the evening sunshine, as too did the row of empty champagne bottles. I shall never know who paid for them, though almost certainly it was Bernard, who always paid for everything if he possibly could. I know I did not, as before leaving for racing I had decided that it would be tempting fate to take any money for a celebration, and I was practically penniless. The Duke of Norfolk, Her Majesty's Representative, came by as he conscientiously made his final round of the establishment he cared for so devotedly. He gave us a rueful look but did not ask us to hurry up and go home.

Eventually I found my way to my car; it was parked next to

Jakie Astor's who, knowing I was alone, had waited to drive me home guessing I would feel like company. As we drove to London he told me that after he had been waiting for ages he asked my driver how long he was going to give me. My driver had replied "I will give him until nine o'clock and then I will go in and fetch him".

By her victory in the Ribblesdale Park Top had established herself as a top-class staying three-year-old filly, arguably the best in the country. I say arguably, since although Pia had beaten St. Pauli Girl by three-quarters of a length in the Oaks, as opposed to the half-length which Park Top had beaten her by at Ascot, a number of good judges who had seen both races took the view that Park Top had more in hand when winning. Bernard's and my ambition now was to put the matter to the test by taking on Pia at the first opportunity.

The filly had run three races in as many weeks and was due for a break from hard training. In the days following Ascot Bernard gave a lot of thought to Park Top's programme for the rest of the season. He and I agreed that the next main objective should be the Yorkshire Oaks, run at York's famous summer meeting in the third week of August. This is another of the great traditional staying races for three-year-old fillies. We understood that Pia was likely to be in the field. The race was nearly two months ahead, which gave Bernard time to give Park Top an easy, and then bring her back into strong work in time for York.

In order that she should be at her peak for the Yorkshire Oaks Bernard was anxious to give her a preliminary outing two to three weeks beforehand. He wanted an engagement that would not make too great demands on her as she would be in need of the race.

The race chosen was the Brighton Cup, a two-thousand-pounds handicap over a mile and a half at the Sussex seaside course on August 7th. This was a bold, unconventional choice. It is unusual for a filly of classic standard to run in a handicap, at any rate so early in her career for defeat in such a race would affect her value as a brood mare. Handicaps, even when not of the highest class, tend to take more winning than condition races, since usually they are run at a faster pace. The reason for this is that the horses carrying the low weights go off at a crack-ing gallop in the hope that an early strong pace will tell against the better class horses carrying high weights. A good example of this can be found by looking at the time of the mile-and-a-half events at the Epsom Summer Meeting of 1969. Here the winner of the Rosebery Memorial Handicap, run over the Derby and Oaks course, was Five Arrows, a horse of no great consequence who took a time which was two and a half seconds faster than Blakeney's in winning the Derby, and two seconds faster than that of Sleeping Partner the Oaks winner. On a calcu-lation that a horse galloping flat out covers a furlong in around twelve seconds. this would mean that Five Arrows would have beaten both the Derby and Oaks winners by over twelve lengths allowing three yards for a length. Such a result is inconceivable even bearing in mind that Five Arrows was carrying a stone less than the classic winners. Incidentally, Park Top's time in winning the Coronation Cup over the same course at the same meeting was the fastest of all, being three-quarters of a second better than Five Arrows.

I should, perhaps, emphasise here the difference between condition races and handicaps. In the former all horses of a said age are allocated the same weight, with colts carrying three pounds more than fillies. Additional poundage, known as penal-ties, can be added to the original weight should a horse win one or more races after the date on which entries for the race are made, while a horse that is still a maiden may be allowed a few pounds less. With handicaps on the other hand, within a certain weight range, say nine stone seven pounds to seven stone seven pounds, each horse is allocated the weight which the handicapper considers a horse's past performance merits. Horses who have won a good race, or a number of small ones, are high in the handicap, while those who have achieved little success carry the bottom weights. The object is to produce a race in which, in theory, all the runners finish in line abreast.

Bernard was not frightened of running Park Top in a handicap and so it was the Brighton Cup we decided on.

It is at this point in Park Top's history that I, her doting owner, did a very stupid thing. Nearly everyone in racing is superstitious; this is understandable as luck plays such a vital part in the game. On racing days, race-courses are littered with ladies wearing strange hats that they would not be seen dead in anywhere else, but which they associate with success. Many owners carry or wear something special or pursue a ritual procedure before a race which they hope to win. In my case, from my earliest days as an owner I had sworn to myself that should ever I have the fortune to own a really good horse, I would allow nothing in my power to prevent my seeing it run in every race it took part in. Now, in the summer of 1967, I found myself at last in just such a position. Many weeks before, however, I had arranged to go and stay with some Italian friends in Venice during the first few days of August, and unwisely I stuck to my plan. I like to think good manners played some part in this decision, since it was not until the second half of July that a firm decision to run at Brighton had been taken. Whatever my reasons, I broke my vow.

The results were not to be apparent at once. Park Top, in the words of the telegram Debo sent me from the course, "Won like a champion". Of the race itself there is little to tell. Park Top, carrying eight stone five pounds, beat a field of useful handicappers by a length and a half. For the first time in her racing career she started favourite at six to four, which was in fact a very generous price. It was the first time she had met older horses but she had just the race Bernard wanted as part of her preparation for York three weeks later.

Park Top was now unbeaten in all her four starts. Although only one of these had been a top-class race, she had begun to capture the racing public's imagination. It is a tribute to her personality, her looks and her ability that at the mid-summer ballot of racing journalists for the Horse of the Year award she received nine votes, not a great number but it was remarkable that with her limited racing career she had attracted any.

Park Top continued to thrive and as the York meeting approached the excitement quickened. Pia, the Oaks heroine, was definitely to be in the field so the result could well decide which was the champion staying filly. The race was due to take place on the first day of the meeting, Tuesday, August 22nd. I drove down to Newmarket on the Friday before, arriving at Stanley House in time for evening stables. I had arranged to spend the night with Bernard, see Park Top and my other horses that evening and in the morning watch the filly do her winding-up gallop.

I walked into Bernard's office about 5 p.m. At once I saw that something was wrong. He was talking to his vet, Mr. Rossdale, a man at the very top of his profession. A blind man could have read the anxiety on Bernard's face. They were just finishing their conversation when I arrived and a moment or two later Rossdale left, saying as he went that he would give the horse an injection, and adding that provided she was sound in the morning he suggested she should be given a canter. He had not mentioned the horse's name, but Bernard's face told me all I needed to know. Something was wrong with Park Top.

Sure enough, as Bernard was to explain, the filly had pulled up slightly lame after cantering at exercise that morning. It was not serious but time was desperately short if she was to take her chance at York. This was bad enough, but even worse for me was the injection which at that very moment Mr. Rossdale was giving Park Top. From its name it was clear that the filly was being injected with a substance that contained cortisone. In August 1967 cortisone was a name to strike terror into the hearts of owners and trainers. All that year the racing world had been preoccupied with the famous case of Hill House, a top-class hurdler whose dope test had proved positive after winning the Schweppes Hurdle the previous February. In the end Ryan Price, Hill House's trainer, was entirely vindicated, but the shadow of whether or not his horse had been doped with a cortisone substance hung over his head for many weeks. In August the case was still sub-judice. Now here was I, a Steward of the Jockey Club, being informed that one of my horses due to run in four days time was being injected with a substance containing cortisone.

Later that evening I discussed the matter with Mr. Rossdale and Bernard. The injection Park Top had been given was entirely within the rules of racing, provided its effects had completely worn off by the time the horse took part in a race thus ensuring that the drug could in no way have affected its performance. Rossdale informed me that all traces of the drug would be eliminated within seventy-two hours of the injection. We all did rapid calculations. The race was due to start at 3 p.m. the following Tuesday. It was then 6 p.m. on Friday, so there were ninety-two hours before the race took place.

Bernard was satisfied with this, since it gave nearly twenty-four hours longer than the maximum time estimated by Mr. Rossdale for the effects of the injection to work through the filly. Bernard's first worry was whether the filly would be all right the following morning. Even if she remained sound after her canter, he would have to give her a gallop on the Sunday morning. Only if she was still sound after that could she run on the Tuesday.

He had a desperately worrying three days ahead of him. Even if all went well, Park Top's preparation for what was likely to be the hardest race of her life·had been interfered with at the most critical moment. Mr. Rossdale could do no more than repeat his opinion, based on years of experience, that no trace of the drug would remain in Park Top seventy-two hours after it had been given.

Friday night was not the usual gay affair one was accustomed to when staying at Northmore. We were both preoccupied with our respective problems arising from Park Top's setback. While Bernard was concerned with getting and keeping her sound, yet fit enough to do herself justice in the race, my problem only arose if he was successful in solving his. I had to decide whether to let her run so soon after the injection. Ninety-two hours was too close for comfort to the required seventy-two hours set by Mr. Rossdale. Drugs are incalculable in the duration of their effects. There are exceptions to every rule and no two horses react in the same way to them. No vet, just as no doctor, can be infallible. Such were my thoughts and I went to sleep with the figures seventy-two and ninety-two going round and round in my head.

The next morning Park Top duly had her canter and walked away sound. Bernard was more cheerful at breakfast, but I had almost hoped the lameness would have recurred, thus solving my problem. Before I left I told Bernard of my doubts as to whether the filly should run. As always he was full of understanding, but he felt that if all went well during and after her final gallop on the following morning, Park Top should be allowed to take her chance.

Driving home I decided on my next step; I would seek the advice of Weatherbys. Weatherbys' role in the administration of racing and its relationship to the Jockey Club can be likened to that of the Civil Service to the Government. They provide the officials to run the day-to-day administration of racing. They advise the Stewards of the Jockey Club and in so doing they can call on a vast experience of racing, stretching back for two hundred years. However, they can do no more than offer advice; it is the Stewards, like the Government, who have to take the decisions. Although it was a Saturday evening, I managed to get hold of David Weatherby and put my problem to him. His reply, if anything, made my decision more difficult, though in the end it was decisive. David told me that no matter what advice my vet had given me, should a dope test taken on Park Top after the Yorkshire Oaks prove positive, that is to say a substance other than a recognised normal nutrient be found in her saliva or urine, under the rules of racing she would be considered to have been doped. She would be disqualified from the race and Bernard would have to face the consequences. These might be the ultimate penalty of his being warned off and having his trainer's licence taken away.

I had arranged to ring Bernard the following morning, after Park Top had had her final gallop. This I duly did, to learn that she had come through it with flying colours, although he would not be sure that the trouble had completely disappeared until he had seen the filly at evening stables. I warned Bernard of my increasing doubts as to the wisdom of running and again he was sympathetic. But, provided she was sound that night, he was clearly going to be very disappointed if I did not allow her to run. At the same time he saw my difficulty and recognised the final decision was mine. I told him I would telephone again that night and let him know what I had decided.

It was not an easy decision; obviously the first consideration was the horse herself. This was a problem for Bernard rather than for me, and I knew he would never allow her to run unless he was completely satisfied that she was fit to do herself justice. To run her would not therefore be taking an unjustifiable risk with her future. I was only faced with a problem if Bernard wanted her to run.

Since her victory in the Ribblesdale, I had become emotionally involved with Park Top and her future. To many such a statement must sound at best sentimental and at worst downright silly. After all, I had neither bred nor bought Park Top, had never ridden her, and took no part in her care and training. Yet I cannot describe my feeling for her in other terms.

I desperately wanted to take on Pia and the others at York, so as to give Park Top the chance to prove that she was indeed the champion filly of her year. I wanted her to win the Yorkshire Oaks for her own sake as well as mine. There was also the problem of the interests of all the others involved with the filly. Not only was Bernard desperately keen for Park Top to run but so too would be Maureen, the head lad, the travelling head lad, and everybody at Stanley House. She was after all the stable's champion. There was Russ Maddock to be considered and indeed Mrs. Scott, without whose judgement and wisdom as a breeder there would have been no Park Top.

Against all this was the problem of the cortisone injection. As a Steward of the Jockey Club, my behaviour must be like that of Caesar's wife. There was always the chance that, in spite of Mr. Rossdale's assurances, the dope test would prove positive. The longer I thought about it the clearer the answer became; the circumstances simply did not justify my allowing Park Top to run. Bernard's training licence would be put at risk and should he lose it I would be responsible. From my own point of view, for a horse of mine to have been found to have been doped would spoil racing for me for ever. Looking back on it, eight years later, I see no reason to change my mind over my decision.

There remained the melancholy task of telling Bernard. I more than half hoped the inspection at evening stables would show Park Top to be unsound. However, Bernard told me that evening she was as sound as a bell, so there was to be no easy way out for me. Bernard behaved perfectly; he did not reproach me, he just accepted my decision. I did not envy him passing the news on to the head lad, Maureen, and the rest of the yard. They would have been less than human if they did not regard me as over fussy.

I fear I tried the patience of my friends and acquaintances highly at York Races that week. I told all and sundry of what had happened and asked them whether or not they thought I had done right and what would they have done. They were all very kind but they must have been bored to tears. Like other people's illnesses, other people's racing problems rarely travel well.

As to the race itself, Pia ran disappointingly, finishing last of the six runners. The winner was Palatch by the French sire Match out of a Palestine mare. The filly had run unplaced in the Oaks, but prior to that had won the Musidora Stakes at the York Spring Meeting where Pia had been third. Palatch did not run again until 1968, but as a four-year-old was second when taking on colts in both the Yorkshire Cup and Jockey Club Stakes at Newmarket from her only three starts. Perhaps of greater interest to this story was the second, Cranberry Sauce, who was beaten by a neck. Caramel, whom Park Top had beaten at Newbury in June, provides a line between Cranberry Sauce and my filly, since the former had also beaten Caramel in the Spring. Looking at the form of the two races there can have been very little between Cranberry Sauce and Park Top. At the time we were sure our filly would have won. With hindsight I am not so certain. Cranberry Sauce proved herself to be a very good filly and in the Free Handicap for three-year-olds compiled at the end of the season she was put two pounds above Park Top.

We now had to plan Park Top's programme for what was left of the season. The obvious alternatives were the Park Hill Stakes on September 15th, at Doncaster, run over the St. Leger distance of one mile six furlongs and a hundred and thirty-two yards, a race often called "The Fillies' St. Leger", and the Prix Vermeille at Longchamp over the shorter distance of a mile and a half, to be run ten days later than the Park Hill. The Vermeille was and is by far the more valuable race; indeed it is the richest race for three-year-old fillies in Europe. In 1967 it was worth over £41,000 to the winner, compared with the £28,000 of that year's English Oaks, while the Park Hill was worth only £2,300. These figures give a fair example of the difference in stake money between France and England.

On every count the Vermeille seemed the more attractive proposition. We knew Park Top stayed a mile and a half, while we could not be sure she would get the extra two and a half furlongs of the Park Hill. The prestige, to say nothing of the prize money involved, in winning the Vermeille was infinitely greater than the Doncaster race.

I was thrilled at the prospect of having a runner at Longchamp at all, let alone in such a famous race as the Vermeille. It was to be the first of Park Top's seven visits to the famous Paris race-course. Her first appearance there was to give no indication of the fame she was later to achieve on the track in the Bois de Bologne.

That month I had been in Austria and arrived in Paris to meet Debo and Bernard two days before the great day. Park Top had travelled well, but Bernard was not entirely happy. He kept saying that her coat was losing its summer gloss, a sign that a horse may be past its peak for the year. Early on the morning of the day before the race, we went down to see the filly being led out for exercise. Russ Maddock was with us and we discussed his riding tactics. Longchamp, like Ascot, is a right-handed course with a short straight; it has a sharp downhill final bend which is made worse by the camber going the wrong way, i.e. sloping outwards. It was clear that Russ would have to be lying close up coming down the hill to the final turn to hold a winning chance.

In the race all Bernard's fears that the dulling of her coat boded ill for her chances were vindicated. She ran badly, never holding out any hope of being concerned in the finish. It was the only time she ran unplaced at Longchamp.

Although on this visit to Paris she lost her unbeaten record and the whole expedition had been disappointing, it brought home to me just what strides Park Top had made during her three-year-old career. It was a far cry from the Mar Lodge Plate at Windsor, in the May twilight, to running against the best fillies in Europe in the Prix Vermeille at Longchamp. She had climbed many rungs up the ladder of fame. Her sparkling victory in the Ribblesdale at Royal Ascot remained a memory untarnished by her running in Paris.

Park Top was now retired for the season. She had had only five races in her life, and she had proved herself good enough to keep in training as a four-year-old.

In the three-year-old Free Handicap drawn up at the end of the season she was allocated eight stone seven pounds, a stone below Royal Palace, the winner of the Derby. She was rated fifth-best filly of the year and fifteenth-best three-year-old. Had she run and won in the Yorkshire Oaks, this assessment would have been different, as both Palatch and Cranberry Sauce were above her in the handicap. The drama of the Yorkshire Oaks and Park Top's failure in the Vermeille showed that the fates were taking their vengeance on me for breaking my vow by missing the Brighton Cup.

It was not until July of the following year that I fully realised the extent to which I had offended the Gods of Racing. Then, to my lasting shame, I lost faith in my heroine. But all this lay in the future. For the present, I could look back on a wonderful year as the proud owner of a top-class and great-hearted filly.

1968
The Brighton Challenge Cup and the Prix d'Hedouville

Park Top came through the winter satisfactorily and Bernard had her well forward in condition by the early spring. Her racing season, though, started off with a miscalculation, resulting in a performance in which she was not to show at her best. Her first race, on the opening day of the Newmarket Guineas Meeting in 1968, was the valuable Totalisator Spring Handicap over one mile. Although she showed up well for three-quarters of the journey the leaders went too fast for her in the closing stages. A mile was clearly too short for her stamina to come into play. She was by no means disgraced, finishing eighth in a high class field of twenty-one, carrying the top weight of nine stone five pounds. The bookmakers paid her the compliment of making her favourite at 100-30, with 8-1 the field bar her. There was no reason to suppose, that given a longer trip she would not be as good as ever, and we were not therefore unduly disappointed.

For her second race Bernard decided on the Ormonde Stakes at the big Chester Spring Meeting, ten days after the Newmarket race. The Ormonde is a condition race of just over a mile and five furlongs for four-year-olds and upwards. It has a long history and has been won by some very good horses. In 1968 it attracted a field of only three, all four-year-olds, Park Top, Starry Halo, Hopeful Venture. Starry Halo belonged to David Robinson and was by Aureole out of a Shantung II mare. The race was his first run of the season. The previous year he had won the Blue Ribbon Trial Stakes at the Epsom Spring Meeting and the Coventry Stakes at Kempton. These were his only two successes, although he had been considered good enough to run in both the Two Thousand Guineas and the Derby. The third runner, Hopeful Venture, was bred by the National Stud, being by Aureole out of a Supreme Court mare. This colt was leased to Her Majesty the Queen and trained by Noel Murless. Hopeful Venture did not run as a two-year-old; at three he won his opening race, the Wood Ditton Stakes, over a mile at the Newmarket Craven Meeting, and followed by winning the Grosvenor Stakes at this same Chester meeting. He was then beaten by a short head by Mariner in the King Edward VII Stakes at Royal Ascot in which Starry Halo finished fourth, less than a length behind. There followed victories in the mile and a half Princess of Wales Stakes at the Newmarket July Meeting and in the rather longer Oxfordshire Stakes at Newbury, the race whose 1968 running was to play an important part in this story. Hopeful Venture was then second, beaten one and a half lengths by Riboco, in the St. Leger. He ended up the season with two runs in France. The first of these, the Prix Henri de Lamarre, he won, beating another English horse, the filly In Command, only to be disqualified and placed second. In his last run of the year he finished unplaced in the valuable Prix de Conseil Municipal, a race of a mile and a half for three-year-olds. As can be seen Hopeful Venture was a top class colt with classic form. He had been given eight stone thirteen pounds in the three-year-old Free Handicap for 1967, eight pounds below Royal Palace and six pounds more than Park Top.

At Chester the race was at level weights except for Park Top being allowed three pounds, the traditional sex allowance. We were therefore meeting Hopeful Venture at three pounds worse terms than on the Free Handicap assessment. Over the years the Free Handicap has proved to be remarkably accurate. In spite of this Bernard was very hopeful that Park Top would win. She had pleased him greatly at home, and the fact that he was more willing to take on the second in the previous year's St. Leger at weight for sex over a distance very close to that of the Doncaster classic shows how highly he regarded her.

The race was to prove both disappointing and unsatisfactory. Three-horse races are notoriously tricky affairs and this was no exception. The going was soft, which we were to learn in the future did not suit Park Top. Hopeful Venture set off in front, with the mare last of the three some way behind. The order remained unchanged until with six furlongs to go Russ made up a lot of ground very quickly, so that Park Top was upsides with Hopeful Venture with more than half a mile to go. Although she was still at his side turning into the short straight, the colt drew clear in the final furlong to win by five lengths, Starry Halo dropping right out of it in the last half mile. Hopeful Venture started an even money favourite, with Park Top thirteen to eight against.

Bernard had to saddle his Derby horse Laureate in the next race, the Dee Stakes, which he duly won, so there was no time for a post mortem on Park Top's performance. It was not until early the following week that we discussed it. We both felt that Russ might have made an error of judgement in making up so much ground so quickly when there were still six furlongs to go. By doing so he had used up the priceless asset of Park Top's tremendous burst of speed before the race entered its vital stages. Against this was the fact that Hopeful Venture had already proved himself a very good staying colt, and in fact went on to win the Hardwicke Stakes at Royal Ascot, and the Grand Prix de Saint-Cloud.

Both Bernard and I now began to have nagging doubts that perhaps our champion was not quite as good as we had thought.

We had to face the fact that she had been well beaten in her last three races. In the meantime Bernard decided to rest her as she had had two hard races inside a fortnight. He also wanted time to think about her future.

She did not reappear on the race-course until the middle of July. This was partly due to the difficulty of finding suitable races for her. Owing to her three-year-old exploits she was set to carry very high weights in handicaps, while her easy defeat by Hopeful Venture indicated she was not good enough for top-class condition races, and her Ribblesdale victory made Park Top ineligible for the more modest races of this type. In the end it was decided to run her in the Magnet Cup, a valuable sponsored handicap run at York on July 13th over one mile two and a half furlongs. She was set to carry top weight of nine stone four pounds.

Her chief opponent seemed to be Game All, a four-year-old mare who in her only two races that season had won a mile and a quarter handicap at Saint-Cloud in France. In the York race Park Top was set to give her six pounds. Another obvious danger was the three-year-old Big Hat, by High Hat, who had been second in another sponsored handicap over a mile and a half at Newcastle in May and who had won three times as a two-year-old. He was set to carry eight stone twelve pounds. In addition there was the six-year-old Farm Walk who had won seven races in his career, including some good handicaps. In his last run he had been third in the Northumberland Plate to Amateur, trained by Bernard for Lord Derby. Farm Walk had been given eight stone thirteen pounds. Also worthy of mention was Castle Yard, a five-year-old gelding belonging to The Queen and trained by Cecil Boyd-Rochfort, who had won the Zetland Gold Cup over a mile and a half on his last appearance. Our mare was set to give him fifteen pounds. Although she was running in handicap company, Park Top had no easy task and a win in the Magnet would at once polish up her somewhat tarnished reputation.

To our dismay, it was not to be. For the second time I was unable to see her run. This time, however, I did not fear the vengeance of the gods, as I had promised many months before to give away the prizes at a girls' school in Harrogate on the day of the race. Harrogate was tantalizingly close to York but the times could not be made to fit and that was that.

The race was broadcast and I asked my driver Joe Oliver to listen to it on the car's radio. I duly gave away the prizes and made a speech even more banal than usual, my mind being thirty miles away to the east on York's Knavesmire. I then bid a hasty goodbye to my hosts and hurried to the car. One look at Joe's face told me all I needed to know, Park Top had not finished in the first three. Joe told me that she had not been mentioned in the commentary until the closing stages of the race but he thought she had finished well up in the field.

Debo had gone to York and returned with a story somewhat similar to that of Chester. Park Top had again run an unsatisfactory race, and Bernard was again inclined to be critical of the way Russ had ridden her. She had been ninth of the ten runners turning into the long straight where she had run wide. The mare then made up a lot of ground in a short distance but her big weight and the amount of ground she had to make up on the leaders proved beyond her. As at Chester, she had had to use up her speed to get into a challenging position and had nothing in reserve for the finish. In the end she was fifth, about five lengths behind the winner Farm Walk, with Castle Yard second. The bookmakers again flattered her by making her favourite at three to one. In fairness to Russ, it must be pointed out that Farm Walk was behind him turning into the straight and was able to go on and win from there. What became apparent was that Park Top was a difficult horse to ride. She took time to warm to her work and therefore had to be waited with and then come from behind. This problem was to remain all her racing days and indeed it was to prove her undoing on the most important day of her life.

We were now back where we were after Chester. Her Magnet Cup running seemed to confirm what we had feared, she was too high even in the best class handicaps, and yet not good enough to win good condition races. Or so we thought at the time.

Now came the moment of my betrayal. My thoughts turned to making money out of Park Top. This was perhaps not quite as bad as it sounds. Owning race-horses is a very expensive hobby. I had been at it for twenty years. I had never previously owned a horse which when sold had fetched even half what I had paid for it. I dreaded to think how much money my racing had cost. There were times when I bitterly reproached myself for squandering money on horses, when it could have been spent in far more responsible ways. Should I not now cash Park Top and at least get back a worthwhile proportion of what I had spent on racing? These were my thoughts, though they made pretty good nonsense of my feelings of emotional involvement with Park Top during the days of her triumphs the previous season. My affections were clearly fickle.

I talked it over with Bernard and he did not deny the strength of the argument of selling the mare. Accordingly word was put round the bloodstock agencies that, provided the price was right, the brilliant but latterly disappointing Park Top was for sale. Offers were not long in coming in. The best was for £30,000 from France; sadly, and against my better judgement, I agreed and the deal was all but completed.

Then came the second tremendous stroke of luck in my ownership of Park Top. A week after the Magnet Cup, I was staying with Bernard for Newmarket races. Anyone who ever had the good fortune to stay with him at Northmore will know of his princely hospitality. When dining with Bernard, even a lifelong member of the Band of Hope would surely succumb to the delights of his cellar; I was no such member and that particular night I had succumbed to no mean tune. After dinner a telephone call from France came through for Bernard. Listening, it became clear that the caller was involved with the sale of Park Top. After a few minutes' conversation, Bernard came over to where I was sitting to tell me that the French dealer who was handling the buyer's side of the transaction wanted an additional five per cent commission to that already agreed. It is well known that alcohol in liberal doses can affect a man in a variety of ways. He can become jovial or markedly bellicose. The Fates decreed that it should be the latter which I was to adopt that evening. Bernard heard me out and then asked "Do you really mean that, Andrew?" "Of course I mean it." Yet it might so easily have gone the other way and instead of adopting a hostile attitude, I might have been filled with the love of my fellow men and greeted the French dealer's request with such comments as "Why not – what's fifteen hundred smackers between friends – bonne chance à lui – vive la France, vive l'entente cordiale – yes of course he can have another five per cent – the best of luck to him". But that night Mars was in the ascendent over Venus. I suppose Bacchus should really take the credit. It was he who had done the trick. The sale was finally and definitely off, and only on the strength of a badly timed telephone call.

History was to show that Park Top's disappointing performance in the Magnet Cup was the nadir of her fortunes. In her remaining sixteen races she was never again to be out of the first three.

The problem now was to find a suitable race for her, a race

she should win without too much difficulty and thus restore her confidence. Among the racing fraternity there are a number of well-known recipes for changing a run of bad luck, some more colourful than others. In Park Top's case, the magic formula was to pay a return visit to Brighton.

She had once again been entered for the Brighton Cup and it seemed sensible to take her back there for a race on a course and over a distance at which she had previously been successful.

Her task was much harder than in the previous year. As a three-year-old she had been set to carry eight stone two pounds, four pounds more than she would have been asked to bear in a weight-for-age race of that distance in August. Now as a four-year-old she had been allotted nine stone ten pounds, thirteen pounds more than weight-for-age. The handicapper had estimated she was a nine pounds better horse as a four-year-old than she had been at three.

After Russ's unhappy rides on the mare in the Ormonde and the Magnet Cup, Bernard and I decided regretfully that it was time to make a change of jockey. Geoff Lewis was offered the mount and accepted.

The value of the race had fallen from the previous year and was now worth £1,500 to the winner. The opposition was what might be expected in a race of its type and value. They were a tough consistent field of second-class handicappers. The best of them was a nine-year-old gelding called Santaway, trained by the late George Todd. Over the years, this horse had won ten races; in his last outing he had run a respectable third in a similar handicap at Ascot Heath. The other main danger appeared to be the four-year-old Lexicon, who had finished fourth in the City and Suburban, beaten just over a length carrying eight stone thirteen. Lexicon had also finished second in the Time Form Anniversary Cup over a mile and a quarter at Sandown, a race in which Santaway had finished nine lengths away

49

fifth. In spite of this, Santaway came into the betting at seven to four favourite with Park Top at three to one and Lexicon eight to one. Park Top hardened in the market to two to one while Santaway drifted slightly. At the off, they were joint favourites at two to one.

I did not repeat the error of the previous year, this time preferring the seaside at Brighton to the Lido in Venice. It was a cold day, with intermittent rain. In the field of nine Park Top was never far behind the leaders. Turning into the straight, with three furlongs to run, Lewis had her third just alongside Lexicon, with Santaway in the lead. Park Top struck the front rather more than a furlong out and running on won by one and a half lengths from Santaway, with Lexicon six lengths away third. Park Top had been going like a winner throughout the race and there had been no doubt about the result throughout the last half mile.

It was a fine performance, since she was giving Santaway twenty-four pounds and Lexicon twelve pounds. The time was exceptionally fast, being three seconds below the average while all the other races run that day, except one, had been run in times well above the average.

Geoff was delighted, expressing the view that Park Top was the best mare he had ever ridden. Bernard and I were over the moon, the jinx had been broken at last, and our champion had once more resumed her rightful place in the winner's enclosure.

Confidence having once more returned, we decided to run her at Newbury in the Oxfordshire Stakes over a mile and five furlongs. Unfortunately I had promised on that day to visit a cousin who was commanding his regiment in Germany, to open a new NAAFI which he had been kind enough to call the Devonshire Arms.

On such occasions the interests of the horse must come before the convenience of the owner. Both Bernard and I wanted

Park Top to run in this particular race since it was certain to be highly competitive and would tell us a lot about her true ability. In this we were not mistaken.

The Oxfordshire Stakes was one of the most important and informative races of Park Top's career. A close analysis of its result tells a great deal about her. Horse-racing can hardly be described as a cerebral activity, nevertheless the performances of top-class horses racing against each other can take on a mathematical interest. Certainly the data to be gleaned from the result of this race proved to be of the greatest value in assessing Park Top's merits. There were ten runners; two six-year-olds, March Parade and Easter Island, neither of whom were of much account; and three four-year-olds besides Park Top. One of these was Dancing Moss, by Ballymoss out of a mare by the American sire Native Dancer. The race was his first of the season, but as a three-year-old he had shown some very useful form when winning the Jockey Club Cup over two miles at Newmarket. He had also finished second in the Irish St. Leger and third, beaten by two short heads, in the 1967 King Edward VII Stakes at Royal Ascot. That race had been won by Mariner, with Hopeful Venture second. Another of the four-year-olds was Fortissimo, who had run third to Hopeful Venture and Tapis Rose in the Hardwicke Stakes at Royal Ascot, also over a mile and a half, beaten three and a half lengths by the winner. Thus, through the Ormonde Stakes running, these two horses were superior to Park Top. As three-year-olds both horses were trained in Ireland, but Dancing Moss was now with Sam Armstrong at Newmarket. The five three-year-olds were headed by Mount Athos, a colt by Sunny Way out of a Telegram mare, thus being entirely French bred. Mount Athos was a top class colt who, after running third to Sir Ivor and Connaught in the Derby, had won the Gordon Stakes at Goodwood and the Princess of Wales Stakes at Newmarket, both over a mile and a half.

In the three-strong Irish contingent, Paddy Prendergast had sent over Canterbury, by Charlottesville out of a Chanteur mare, and therefore likely to stay for ever. He had won his previous race, worth over £1,500 at Navan, a big stake for Ireland in 1968. Paddy's other charge Young Alexander was there to make the running for Canterbury. The third was Levmoss, owned and trained by Seamus McGrath. This horse, who was to play such a vital part in the crisis of Park Top's racing career, is interestingly bred, being by the miler Le Levanstell out of a Ballymoss mare, a pedigree combining great stamina with great speed. The combination is the same but the opposite way round to that of Park Top, whose stamina came from her sire and her speed from her dam. Prior to running in the Oxfordshire Stakes Levmoss had given no indication that he was in the top class. He had run fourth in the Queen's Vase over two miles at Royal Ascot, before which he had also been fourth to Laureate – in Bernard's view not a classic horse – in the Lingfield Derby Trial Stakes. Levmoss's only victory had been in a small race at Phoenix Park, Dublin, back in May. The remaining runner St. Patrick's Blue, owned by the Queen, appeared to be outclassed.

As in other condition races the weights for the Oxfordshire Stakes are based on the weight-for-age table. This was established many years ago and is a formula under which horses of different ages are allocated varying weights according to the distance of the race and the time of the year at which it is run. In August, over a mile and a half, three-year-olds are set to carry eight stone three, four-year-olds nine stone, while five-year-olds and upwards are given one pound more. Under the conditions of the race, runners who had won one or more valuable races had to carry penalties. The actual weights carried in the race were as follows: Park Top, Dancing Moss and Fortissimo nine stone three pounds, March Parade and Easter Island nine stone, Mount Athos eight stone nine pounds, and the remaining three-year-olds eight stone three. Brian Taylor, riding Levmoss, carried one pound overweight, so that the horse actually carried eight stone four pounds.

Since the distance was just over a furlong further than one and a half miles, it is not possible to relate the weights carried exactly to the weight-for-age formula. But working to the weight scale for a mile and a half race in August it will be seen that Park Top was meeting all her opponents except Mount Athos at several pounds worse than the weight-for-age scale, taking the three pound allowance into account.

The going was soft, putting stamina at a premium at the expense of speed. Mount Athos started at 2-1 favourite, with Park Top at 3-1, which seemed on her recent running and considering the quality of the field an ungenerous price. Canterbury was backed down from 9-2 to 7-2, with Levmoss virtually unconsidered at 100-6.

Young Alexander duly made the running for more than a mile when Canterbury took over. Turning into the straight, with half a mile to go, Levmoss had been lying fifth just ahead of Park Top. Brian Taylor on Levmoss challenged Canterbury inside the distance, getting up in the last few strides to win by a neck. Lewis, who again had the ride on Park Top, had her beautifully placed with two furlongs to run and although she ran on well she could not quite catch the leading pair, being beaten another neck in third place, with the fourth horse Dancing Moss six lengths behind. Mount Athos finished sixth, rather more than two lengths behind Dancing Moss, with Fortissimo between them.

While this desperate finish was taking place, I was far away in Germany watching an Army polo match. Michael Wyatt, whose regiment was serving in the vicinity, had arranged a wireless link between the polo ground and Newbury racecourse, so he was able to tell me within a matter of seconds of the finish of the race that there was a photo finish. Some few minutes later he brought me the details of the result.

On getting back to England, Bernard and I analysed the result. Although the mare had beaten Mount Athos comfortably, the outcome of the race seemed disappointing. It was true that at strict weight-for-age rather than the actual weights carried, Park Top would have narrowly defeated Levmoss and Canterbury, but the form of these two horses at the time did not appear to amount to much. Bernard did say that Paddy Prendergast thought very highly of Canterbury, a fact borne out by his provision of a pacemaker and the heavy support for him in the ring. Canterbury was to run next in the St. Leger some three weeks later.

We also had to bear in mind that the soft going was against Park Top. She needed fast ground to show her brilliant speed to its greatest advantage. However, Bernard was sufficiently pleased with the mare's performance to suggest another journey to Longchamp, this time for the Prix d'Hedouville over a mile and three and a half furlongs, to be run on Sunday September 8th. The alternative was the Peter Hastings Stakes at Newbury over a mile and a quarter to be run on September 14th.

It was a relatively easy decision to reach. By her running in the Oxfordshire Stakes, Park Top had shown she was a genuine stayer so the longer distance of the d'Hedouville would probably suit her better. In addition, the French race was worth half as much again as that at Newbury. As it turned out, it was not only the right decision but a lucky one as the Peter Hastings had to be abandoned because the race-course became waterlogged just before it was due to take place.

So almost exactly a year after Park Top's first disappointing visit to Longchamp, Bernard and I again set off for Paris. Park Top, accompanied by Maureen and Michael Ryan, then Bernard's travelling head lad, had flown over two days earlier. Over the next two years I was to grow accustomed to the cycle of emotion that preceded Park Top's appearances at the great centre of European racing in the Bois de Bologne.

In the days leading up to the race, the excitement would mount steadily, accompanied by moments of acute anxiety whenever the telephone rang for fear it was Bernard to say that the mare had suffered some injury. Once in Paris apprehension gradually took over. This in turn grew and grew until the race started, by which time any hope of success had entirely evaporated.

Awaking early on the Sunday morning, I began to wish we had chosen a less ambitious race. Park Top appeared to have no such worries and as usual had travelled splendidly and looked magnificent. Unlike the previous autumn, her bay coat still carried a glorious summer bloom.

Over breakfast, armed with *Paris Sport*, we assessed the strength of the opposition. There was a field of six, the best of the French-trained contingent being two four-year-old colts Beau Paon and Bagdad. The former, before running disappointingly the week before in the Prix Henri Foy, which is one of the main trials for the Arc de Triomphe, had won the valuable and prestigious Prix Maurice de Nieuil at Saint-Cloud over an extended mile and a half in July. Bagdad had only run once previously as a four-year-old, coming third in a high-class mile and a half event at Saint-Cloud back in May. He had been a really good three-year-old, winning the Prix Conseil Municipal the previous autumn. Among those he had beaten were: Samos, the winner of the Prix Royal-Oak, the French equivalent of the St. Leger; Dan Kano, winner of the Irish St. Leger and the Grand Prix de Vichy, as well as the Ulster Derby; and our old foe Hopeful Venture. The only three-year-old in the field was the lightly raced Right Honourable. In his previous race he had been beaten half a length by the English-trained Wolver Hollow over

55

a mile and a quarter at Deauville. Wolver Hollow was another horse we were to hear a lot about in the following year.

The other English challenger was the four-year-old Tiber, by Hugh Lupus from a Chamossaire mare. This colt was owned by John Margadale and trained by Jeremy Tree. In his previous race he had put up a magnificent performance in the Johnny Walker Ebor Handicap at York, when carrying eight stone eleven he had been beaten by a neck by Alignment, no mean performer himself, Tiber had been giving the latter seventeen pounds, a tremendous amount of weight to give away over a mile and three quarters on the Knavesmire. Tiber had also won a valuable mile and a half handicap under eight stone eight at Haydock. Jeremy had got Lester Piggott to ride his colt, and made no secret that he fancied his chance.

Of the race there is little to tell; the drama came afterwards. Geoff Lewis again had the mount and he settled the mare as usual in the rear of the small field. He bided his time until well into the straight and then pounced. It was all over in a few strides. Park Top's great speed carried her to the front rather more than a furlong out and she won hard held by a length and a half from Beau Paon, who beat Bagdad a short head for second place. Tiber was fourth, but Jeremy thought his horse had been unlucky in not getting a clear run in the straight.

We hurried down the stands to the unsaddling enclosure. Our jubilation was short-lived, however, for just as Geoff was dismounting and we were crowding round, all talking at once, the hooter sounded denoting a Stewards' Enquiry into the result. Its loud and menacing wail had much the same effect on us as did the air raid sirens over London during the Blitz.

A feeling of deep dismay overcame us. Neither Bernard nor I had seen anything wrong, but my glasses had been far from steady once the horses had entered the straight. Geoff hurried off to the Stewards' room while we were left waiting in an agony of doubt. Only those who have undergone the experience can know of the torture of hanging about for the result of an enquiry or objection in a race in which one owns the winner. Like everything else in racing it is of course all out of proportion, a race is only a race and if it is lost in the Stewards' room it is not the end of the world. At the time, it does not seem like that. On that Sunday afternoon in the Bois, Bernard and I had as unpleasant a few minutes as I care to remember. We kept on telling each other that the mare could not have interfered with any other runner and that it was going to be all right, but as the minutes dragged by, so my conviction that Park Top would lose the race grew.

In the end all was well. A kind official told us that there was no alteration to the original placings, so Park Top had won the first of her great Longchamp victories. My joy at winning overcame my dislike of telephoning from a call box and I rang Debo at Chatsworth with the news. Park Top's victory in this race had given me more pleasure than anything since the Ribblesdale.

To make everything perfect, Bernard won the next race, too, with a four-year-old colt of Walter Berman's called Petros. At the end of the season this colt and Park Top were both given nine stone thirteen in the French Free Handicap, but I believe Bernard would have greatly fancied my mare to beat the colt at level weights.

Four days later at Doncaster, Canterbury was beaten a short head by Ribero in the St. Leger. This Ribot colt had won the Irish Sweeps Derby, beating Sir Ivor the Epsom Derby winner by two lengths (although the latter was to reverse the placings when finishing second to Vaguely Noble in the Arc de

Triomphe). Canterbury's running in the last of the classics proved beyond doubt that Park Top's win in the d'Hedouville had not been a fluke.

On returning to Newmarket from France Park Top seemed as full of herself as ever. Bernard therefore felt it would not be asking too much of her to give her one more race before the end of the season. In retrospect this decision looks greedy; perhaps it was. In mitigation of our decision, at the time we thought that the race we chose, the Cumberland Lodge Stakes at Ascot, would be the last race of Park Top's career and that she would be sent to stud after it. I was very keen for her to run as on her recent form she had an outstanding chance of winning. I realised that Park Top was likely to be the best horse I would ever own, and I wanted to make the most of her ability.

The Cumberland Lodge is a condition race for three-year-olds and upwards over a mile and a half, and a valuable race by English standards.

There were only five runners, of which the chief danger was another four-year-old, Chicago, by Fidalgo, owned and bred by Gerry Oldham, and trained by Harry Wragg at Newmarket.

Chicago's racing career was to be intimately concerned with that of Park Top. His training is an admirable example of Harry Wragg's method of training a good horse. He shows infinite patience, introducing even those of whom he has a high opinion at a comparatively low level, gradually letting the horses develop their full potential. Chicago ran once as a two-year-old, being placed. As a three-year-old he won his first race, the Condor Stakes for maidens over a mile at Nottingham, a race worth less than £500. There followed a disappointing run behind Tiber, another horse of whom we have heard and will hear of again, in a valuable mile and a quarter handicap at Newcastle, for which he started second favourite. His trainer then dropped him in class and he won a minor mile and a half event at Beverley in June. He did not win again as a three-year-old, although on the strength of his being placed second to the five-year-old Farm Walk in the Vaux Gold Tankard at Redcar, Chicago started favourite for the Ebor Handicap. Both in that race and in his last appearance of the season he ran disappointingly. His first two runs as a four-year-old also gave no hint of things to come, since he ran unplaced in a very ordinary handicap over a mile and a half at Sandown in April, and followed this by being nowhere in a valuable Apprentice Handicap at York in May over the same distance.

After this his trainer's patience showed dividends as the horse won his next three races, beginning with a condition race worth £800 over a mile and five furlongs at Newbury. There followed another more valuable race of the same kind, the Henry II Stakes over two miles at Sandown. Chicago completed his hat-trick by beating his only rival in the Commonwealth Stakes, again at Sandown, a race it may be remembered won by Park Top's sire, Kalydon.

By this time, Harry Wragg thought enough of the horse to send him to Saint-Cloud for the £14,000 Prix Maurice de Nieuil. Here he finished in the ruck behind Beau Paon. His next race was a second appearance in the Vaux Gold Tankard which again he failed to win, this time finishing fourth, beaten eight lengths by Quartet, but giving the winner, also a four-year-old, seventeen pounds. Next he was sent to Germany for the Grosser Preis von Baden. He ran a fine race, finishing second to Luciano at level weights. The latter was a high class German colt, who in his previous race had won the valuable Grosser Preis von Mordheim Westphalen, beating among others Tiber.

In the previous year Luciano had been second to another good horse of Gerry Oldham's called Salvo, also trained by Harry Wragg. This horse had won the Hardwicke Stakes at Royal Ascot and then finished second to Busted in the King

George VI and Queen Elizabeth Stakes. Thus Harry Wragg clearly knew what he was up against when sending Chicago over to take on Luciano.

Chicago was obviously a very real threat to Park Top in the Cumberland Lodge, but having recently beaten Beau Paon, Chicago's easy conqueror at Saint-Cloud in July, the mare appeared to have the beating of the colt. The rest of the field included Tiber, who Jeremy Tree was hoping would reverse placings with Park Top after his unlucky run in the d'Hedouville. There was also the three-year-old Noblesse Oblige, who had opened his winning account in a maiden race at Doncaster a fortnight earlier. The remaining runner was the six-year-old Midnight Marauder. This was the horse which had beaten both Lexicon and Santaway, second and third to Park Top in the Brighton Cup back in August, in the Time Form Anniversary Cup at Sandown in June.

An examination of the weights carried by the four horses in the two races showed that Park Top should beat Midnight Marauder even without taking into account the improvement she had made since the Brighton race. As always as the moment of the race approached, confidence began to ebb away, but discounting pre-race nerves I was very much hoping that Park Top would retire from racing with a victory over the course and distance that had first proved her to be a really good horse.

My optimism was shared by the betting public who made Park Top 7-4 favourite, with Chicago 5-2 and Tiber 3-1. I had been too optimistic and the race proved to be a bitter disappointment. In fact, looking back on her racing career, Park Top's performance in the 1968 Cumberland Lodge is the most puzzling of her defeats. Midnight Marauder made the running until the field turned into the straight with Noblesse Oblige second, followed by Chicago and then Park Top. As Midnight Marauder fell away Noblesse Oblige took over. Geoff Lewis on the mare made his challenge immediately afterwards and quickly took the lead with more than a furlong to run. From the sands it looked all over bar the shouting. Suddenly, the whole situation changed. Park Top seemed to stop to nothing and Chicago swept by her inside the last furlong to win easily by four lengths, with Tiber five lengths further back third.

Taken by itself, Park Top had been far from disgraced since, taking sex allowance into account, she was giving the winner six pounds. However, the way she stopped when the race appeared at her mercy was a great blow. There could be no question of her not staying the distance. It is true the going was heavy which was against her but she had run a far better race on similar ground in the Oxfordshire Stakes. Furthermore she had showed all her great acceleration when taking the lead from Noblesse Oblige early in the straight. The only explanation was that after a long season she was 'over the top'.

I blamed myself for running her and wished I had retired her after her Longchamp triumph. Her four-year-old career had ended in the same way as had her three-year-old, with a defeat. Indeed, Park Top's failure in the Cumberland Lodge was a far greater disappointment than that in the Vermeille the previous year. It also had an infinitely greater effect on her racing career. I have said earlier the Ascot race was intended to be her last. However, with her defeat came a return of the feeling that somehow the mare had never quite received her due on the race-course. I thought, as did Bernard, that she was a far better horse than her racing record showed.

There was no immediate change of plan after the disappointment of the Cumberland Lodge. Bernard, Debo and I started discussing suitable stallions to send her to. But a feeling of frustration remained. I also felt something else. I had owned many horses over the years and had won relatively few races. Now that I had a really good race-horse, I wanted to win as many races with her as I possibly could, even if it meant damaging her prospects as a brood mare.

Autumn became winter without a decision as to which horse the mare should be mated with. Finally, in December, Debo made up my mind for me. One evening at Chatsworth after yet another indecisive discussion about possible stallions, she said: "Why don't you keep her in training for another year – you know that is what you want?" She was of course quite right, but I had been too timid to admit it. In the years since Park Top graced the race-course, it has become more common to keep mares in training after the age of four. As I write, those two fabulous race mares Allez France and Dahlia are both still in training at the age of six.

Park Top's success as a five-year-old and to a lesser extent at six may have had something to do with this change of fashion. It is probable that the enormous increase in prize money, particularly in France, has been the real factor. Be that as it may, I was greatly relieved by the decision to keep her in training just as I had been after the evening at Northmore that resulted in cancelling her sale.

I suppose I was again very lucky, although perhaps lucky is not quite the right word to describe a man who takes his wife's advice, particularly when it is of the kind he wants to hear. Where luck undoubtedly played a large part was in the mare's defeat in the Cumberland Lodge. Had she won then, it is reasonable to suppose that I would have stuck to the plan of retiring her to stud. I would not like to be too sure about this. It is possible the prospect of seeing my colours carried by a great horse would have made me change my mind in any case.

1969
The Great Year

The year of 1969, for which we hoped so much, had a most unhappy start. In February Bernard was told that he had cancer
of the jaw. His doctor made him undertake a prolonged period
of radio therapy, after which he had to undergo an operation.
The treatment meant that he had to be in London most days of
the week. A lesser man would have abandoned training horses
for the duration of the treatment. Bernard had other ideas.
Throughout the first three months of the 1969 racing season he
invariably supervised the training of the horses in his charge.
This meant getting up at six in the morning. Then, providing
that the time of his visit to the hospital in London permitted, he
would again go out with his horses after breakfast. The usual
pattern for trainers is to work those horses which are fully fit
before breakfast, and after it those which are in the preliminary
stages of their preparation. In racing jargon these two periods
are known as first and second lots. Either directly after breakfast, or after second lot, Bernard would drive to London for
treatment then return to Newmarket for evening stables. Thus
he was able by a display of immense physical courage and
determination to combine the arduous dedicated work of training with a long period of debilitating treatment. Owing to his
timetable he was not usually able to see his horses run, except
at weekends. All this must have been immensely frustrating, but
he realised that getting his horses ready for their races was
where he played the vital role. The travelling head lad and the

jockey and sometimes television could tell him what happened on the race-course.

The season was to prove outstandingly successful for him as a trainer, and a triumph for him as a man. When racing came to an end Bernard finished third in the list of winning trainers, having won in Britain alone forty-one races worth £87,553. In addition, he made a number of highly successful visits to the race-courses of France, and to crown it all he won the Washington Laurel International race in November.

As in many dramas, the opening scene of Park Top's year of glory was in a minor key. During the winter the disappointment of the mare's defeat in the Cumberland Lodge was largely forgotten, while her victory in the d'Hedouville and her fine race in the Oxfordshire Stakes were remembered. Bernard was in no hurry to bring Park Top to full racing pitch. Remembering how disappointingly she had run in her first two races as a four-year-old, he was anxious for the warm weather to arrive before he put Park Top into strong work.

By the beginning of May he was satisfied that she was as good, if not better, than ever. She did, however, give him some anxiety, as each morning walking around the home paddocks at Stanley House before going on to the Heath for her daily canter or gallop she was nearly always slightly lame. The lameness soon wore off, but it was disquieting. It was only with the passing of time and her successful reappearance on the race-course that this early morning lameness ceased to worry Bernard. She was also a victim of Set Fast, a form of equine cramp, after fast work and following her races.

The Coronation Cup over a mile and a half at Epsom was to be her first major objective. Bernard decided to give her one preliminary race before taking on the previous year's classic colts.

Unable to find a suitable race in England he chose the Prix de la Seine at Longchamp for her season's debut. This relatively *(above)* Park Top (Russ Maddock) wins the 1967 Ribblesdale Stakes at Royal Ascot; St Paul's Girl *(left)* was second

(below) The Brighton Cup 1967: Park Top (Russ Maddock) winning from Happy Haven and Grock II

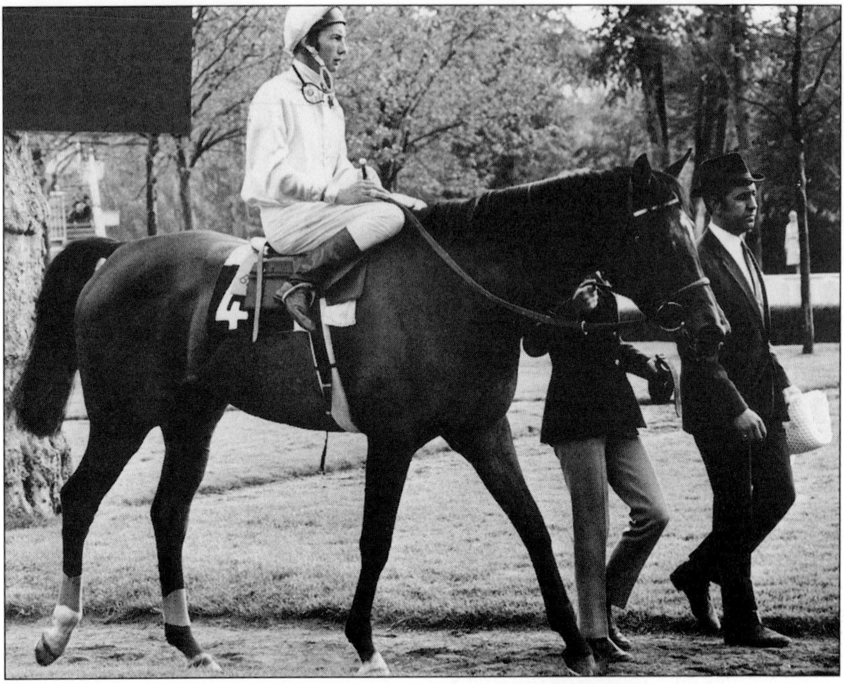

(above) Park Top with Lester Piggott up

(below) Park Top at four with Maureen Foley who cared for her throughout her career

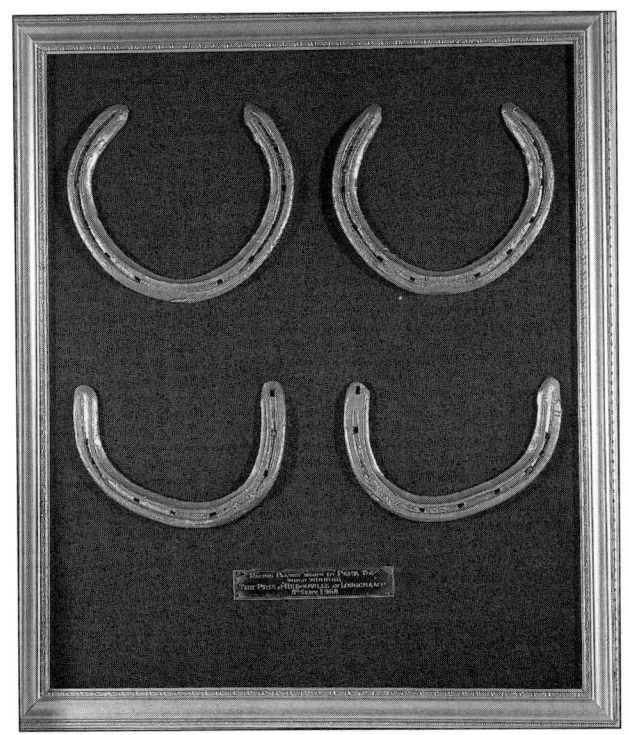

(above) Plates worn by Park Top when winning the
Prix d'Hedouville, September 1968 (note the strange
shape of the near fore shoe which accounted for the
fact that she pulled out fairly lame every morning)

(below) Prix d'Hedouville, Longchamp, 8 September 1968: Park Top (Geoff
Lewis) wins from Beau Paon, Bagdad and Tiber

Consternation after winning the Prix d'Hedouville, 8 September 1968, at Longchamp as the hooter signals a Stewards' enquiry. Happily, Park Top's victory was allowed. *From left to right:* Geoff Lewis, the Duke of Devonshire, Bernard van Cutsem

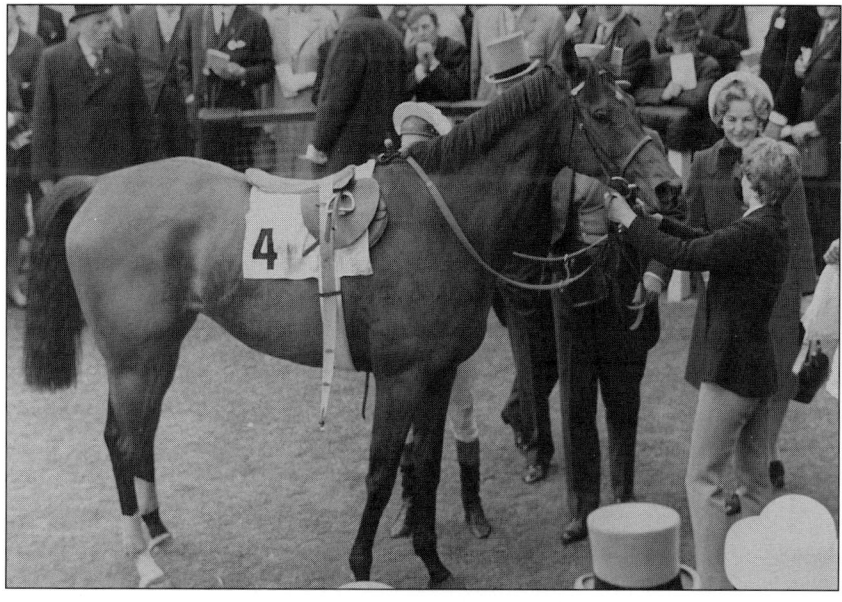

The Coronation Cup, 5 June 1969: *(above)* the finish and *(below)* the winner's enclosure

(above) Park Top with Bernard van Cutsem and Maureen Foley at Stanley House Stables

(below) Park Top (Geoff Lewis) winning the Hardwicke Stakes at Royal Ascot, 20 June 1969. Chicago *(left)* was second

King George VI and Queen Elizabeth Stakes, Ascot, 26 July 1969. Park Top
(Lester Piggott) winning from Crozier (D. Keith) and Hogarth (C. Ferrari)

(above) Hardwicke Stakes, 20 June 1969, Geoff Lewis up

(below) After Park Top won the Prix Foy at Longchamp, 7 September 1969.
Left to right: Michael Ryan, Lester Piggott, the author,
the Duchess of Devonshire, Bernard van Cutsem

(above) Longchamp, Prix la Seine, 22 May 1969: the Duchess of Devonshire,
Lester Piggott and Bernard van Cutsem

(below) Trainer and owner at Longchamp

(above) Longchamp, 7 May 1970, La Coupe, 150 metres before the post.
Left to right: Chaparral, Le Chouan, Park Top (Lester Piggott)

(below) Headlines from 12 October 1970 after disaster at Longchamp

Park Top (Lester Piggott) going down to the start of the
Cumberland Lodge Stakes, 24 September 1970

(above) Maureen Foley and Park Top at Chatsworth, before their appearance at the Bakewell Show on 7 August 1969

Angela Napier and Champion Shetland Pony Easter Bonnet meet Park Top and Maureen Foley late on in 1967

minor race over the same distance as the Coronation Cup was worth £2,600 to the winner, a small stake by French standards though not by English. The race was confined to mares and fillies.

During the winter Bernard and I had many discussions over the question of who was to ride Park Top in the coming season. Geoff Lewis had got on very well with her and was in no way to blame for her defeat in the Cumberland Lodge. However Lester Piggott had shown an interest in her so we decided Bernard should approach him to find out whether he would be willing to ride Park Top in her first outing of 1969. Lester then, as now, was riding as a freelance and able to pick and choose his mounts. Virtually every owner and trainer wanted him to ride their horses, particularly in big races so Bernard and I knew that even if Lester agreed to ride Park Top in her first race he would not commit himself for any future race until he had weighed up the respective chances of the various horses on whom he had been offered the mount. Lester's genius gives him the right to adopt such an attitude but it causes problems for the owner and trainer of a horse which he may or may not decide to ride. They have to calculate the advantage of booking Lester for a ride against the possibility that he may decide at the last moment to switch to another horse, by which time the remaining top-flight jockeys will have already fixed up their mounts.

The Prix de la Seine produced a field of six, out of which only one appeared at all dangerous. This was the four-year-old Pandora Bay. She had been a good filly as a three-year-old following in Park Top's steps by winning the Ribblesdale the year after the mare's triumph. She had also been third in the Oaks and the Cheshire Oaks. As a three-year-old she had been trained by Geoffrey Barling but during the winter had been sent over to France. The other four runners were of not great account. We therefore knew that the ideas we were entertaining of running

the mare in the Coronation Cup would be only a pipe dream unless she won the Longchamp race convincingly.

Unfortunately I could not go over to France to see her run.
Many weeks earlier I had arranged to be host at a reception
given by the Association of Municipal Corporations, of which
I was then President. The AMC was an august body, now de-
funct, consisting of Mayors, Town Clerks and other leaders in
local government throughout England and Wales. In missing
the Prix de la Seine I did not feel I was tempting the Fates of
racing as when I went to Venice rather than Brighton back in
1967. The circumstances were similar to when I had to miss
the Magnet Cup owing to the prize-giving at the school in
Harrogate; I was fulfilling an engagement which I had been
honoured and flattered to receive. To my superstitious mind, to
have thrown over the function at the last moment so as to go
racing would have been the more likely way to annoy the gods.
My visit to Venice had been in search of pleasure, my presence
at the AMC party was merely showing common courtesy to
those who had paid me a compliment. At least I was spared the
agonising hours leading up to the off. It would have been a
nerve-racking time, since although it was not an important race
in itself there was an enormous amount at stake. If Park Top
failed to win then I had made a grave error of judgement in
keeping her in training. Furthermore, all our grandiose hopes
of her running against the top-class colts at Epsom would
vanish.

I went to my party about 5.00 p.m. without knowing the
result of the race. There followed a good illustration of the vast
interest in racing that is shown in all walks of life in this country. My guests that evening, although distinguished, were somewhat prosaic, not at all the kind of people one would expect to
take a keen interest in the Turf. At least that was what I
thought, but not a bit of it; among the first half-dozen guests to

arrive was a Town Clerk from the Midlands who congratulated me warmly on the success of my horse in Paris. I could not believe my ears. I thought at first that he must be referring to Park Top's win the previous autumn. But no, he was a keen follower of racing and a great supporter of the mare. Knowing he would meet me at the party he had taken the trouble to ring up the Press Association to find out the result of her race that afternoon. The evening that I had been regarding as duty at once became a celebration. Bernard had so arranged his radio therapy treatment to enable him to go over to Paris. Later that night I talked to him on the telephone. He was delighted with the mare's performance – she had done everything he had expected of her. Lester was equally enthusiastic and had agreed to ride her in the Coronation Cup. He is reported to have remarked to Bernard on dismounting after the race: "Where have you been keeping this one?"

The days between the Prix de la Seine and the Coronation Cup were similar to those between the Twyford Stakes and the Ribblesdale two years before. Rising excitement as the day of the race got closer, anxiety every time the telephone rang for fear it was Bernard with bad news about Park Top. By the time the Monday of Epsom week arrived apprehension had taken over. The prospect of success receded as the day of the race approached. Fortunately, the Derby being run on the Wednesday, the day before the Coronation Cup, there was all the interest and excitement inspired by the world's greatest race to occupy one's mind. The race had an added interest for all concerned with Park Top since, provided she fulfilled our hopes in the Coronation Cup, she was likely to meet those who ran best in the Derby later in the summer in such races as the King George VI and Queen Elizabeth Stakes at Ascot, and possibly in the Eclipse at Sandown. In the event, the virulent epidemic of coughing which played such havoc with the middle part of the 1969 season meant that Park Top would not run against Blakeney, the winner, or any of those involved in the Derby until the Arc de Triomphe four months later.

Early on the Thursday, Bernard and I drove down to see Park Top while she was walked out for exercise at the Epsom race-course stables. It was a lovely sunny morning and Park Top looked magnificent. Having seen our champion safely returned to her box, Bernard and I were in good spirits and temporarily full of optimism. We were walking back to the car when we passed Noel Murless escorting Connaught, one of our chief rivals, back to his box. At once our optimism was shattered and we returned to earth with a bang. Noel's four-year-old colt looked a picture, a magnificent specimen of a thoroughbred exuding power and strength. Visibly shaken, we returned to London.

We had always known that this race would be a turning point in Park Top's career. This time, the chips were down with a vengeance.

The Coronation Cup is sandwiched between the Derby and the Oaks at the Epsom summer meeting. It is the most important race of the year over a mile and a half for colts and fillies of four-years-old and upwards and has been won by some of the greatest horses on the Turf. The most recent Derby victor who has gone on to win it is Mill Reef, while in the years immediately prior to Park Top's victory, Royal Palace and Charlottown followed their Derby wins by taking the race the following year. At the beginning of the decade that unforgettable filly of the Aly Khan's Petite Etoile had won the race in successive years. I will return to this brilliant filly later, but for the moment it was the possibility of Park Top being the first mare to win this much-coveted event since Petite Etoile that excited me most when thinking about the race.

Looking back on it, I regret that the winner of the previous

68

year's Derby, Sir Ivor, was not in the field. Had he been, I think Park Top would have beaten him, particularly as the race was run at a tremendous pace. At the time, having to take on the second, third and fourth in the 1968 Derby was sufficiently alarming. These were Connaught, Mount Athos and Remand. Connaught was by the Derby winner St. Paddy. As a two-year-old he had been unplaced in his only race. At three, having refused to enter the stalls in his first race he had run unplaced in the Two Thousand Guineas. A week later he finished second to Remand in the Chester Vase, after which he was second to Sir Ivor in the Derby. Connaught won his first race when taking the mile and a half King Edward VII Stakes at Royal Ascot a fortnight after Epsom. Here he beat Ribero, who was later to win the St. Leger by twelve lengths. At Goodwood, in the Gordon Stakes, Connaught again refused to start, the race being won by Mount Athos. The colt then went to York where he won the Great Voltigeur Stakes over a mile and a half. As a result of this he started eleven to ten on favourite for the St. Leger. Connaught's stamina limitations were shown up in the Doncaster Classic, and he finished a long way behind Ribero.

As a four-year-old Connaught's only appearance so far had been in the Coronation Stakes over a mile and a quarter at Sandown at the end of April. Here he beat Jimmy Reppin by six lengths. This was a fine performance since the latter was a top class miler, finishing third to Sir Ivor and Petingo in the 1968 Two Thousand Guineas.

Park Top had met and beaten Mount Athos in the Oxfordshire Stakes the previous year. In the current season Mount Athos had won a two-mile race at Haydock. This had been his only race prior to coming to Epsom. Remand, owned by my great friend Jakie Astor, was an unlucky horse. He was beautifully bred for stamina and speed, being by the St. Leger winner Alcide out of the good mare Admonish, who was by Palestine, and represented the best of the famous Astor blood lines. As a two-year-old Remand was unbeaten in three starts, winning the Beaufort Plate at Salisbury, the seven-furlong Solario Stakes at Sandown and the one-mile Royal Lodge Stakes at Ascot. Consequently he was given nine stone five in the two-year-old Free Handicap, two pounds below Petingo and a pound less than Vaguely Noble. As we have seen, as a three-year-old he had beaten Connaught in the Chester Vase. This win led him to start second favourite to Sir Ivor in the Derby. Like all his other countless friends at Epsom on that Derby day, my heart bled for Jakie when Remand appeared in the paddock before the race. The horse looked a shadow of what he had been at Chester three weeks earlier. It was clear that all was not well. Jakie would have liked to have withdrawn him but did not do so out of respect to the countless thousands who had already backed him. An owner's responsibility to the betting public has always been a problem. Owning a much-fancied horse in the Derby makes the responsibility particularly heavy as for millions of people it is one of the two races in the year on which they have a bet. In running Remand Jakie added to the great respect he had already earned on the Turf, but the price he had to pay was a stiff one. After the race Remand was found to be running a temperature. The effect of the hard race he had in the Derby compounded the effects of the illness and Remand did not run again that season and it is possible he was never as good a horse again. He had had one outing prior to coming to Epsom, winning the mile and a half Westbury Stakes at Sandown from his pacemaker Hipster, with the six to four on favourite Ribero third. Hipster was again in the field as a pacemaker to Remand. The other three runners were the six-year-old colt Crozier, and the four-year-olds Ribero and the French Val d'Aosta.

Crozier was a tough genuine colt, although not quite in the top class. In his four previous seasons he had won twelve times over distances varying from a mile and a quarter to two miles and a quarter. In all, he ran thirty-six times. His best performances in previous years had been winning the Grand Prix de Vichy and the Jockey Club Cup at Newmarket as a five-year-old, and the Doncaster Cup when a year younger. He had shown that he was as good if not better than ever as a six-year-old by winning earlier in the current season the John Porter Stakes at Newbury. In a driving finish he had been beaten a short head by Fortissimo, but the latter had been disqualified and Crozier awarded the race.

The challenger from France, Val d'Aosta, had finished a long way back behind Carmarthen in the Prix Ganay at Longchamp in April. The previous autumn, however, he had run Chicago to a length in the Gran Premio del Jockey Club over a mile and a half in Milan in receipt of eight pounds. Chicago confirmed this form by beating Val d'Aosta in the £11,000 Premio Roma over a mile and three-quarters, this time with Chicago conceding ten pounds.

Chicago's two wins in Italy after beating Park Top at Ascot in September indicate that he was probably a better horse in the autumn of 1968 than at any time in his career. Val d'Aosta had also been third to Ribero and Sir Ivor in the Irish Sweeps Derby.

In the parade Remand, with Joe Mercer up, looked a different horse than he had on Derby Day twelve months earlier. Collectively they looked a formidable field of colts for Park Top to take on.

The going was perfect, so the ground would be no excuse should Park Top fail. In the betting Park Top opened joint favourite with Connaught at three to one, while Remand was seven to two. Of the others, Crozier and Mount Athos were the best backed at 100-7. In the minutes just before the off there was a flood of money for Remand. As a result, he started clear favourite at 9-4. Park Top hardened slightly to become second favourite at 11-4 with Connaught remaining 3-1. In view of Park Top's chequered career as a four-year-old, and the weakness of the opposition in her only race of the season compared with what she was taking on now, the betting public paid her a compliment in supporting her so strongly. I thought I already had more than enough at stake in the race and did not have a bet. Eventually the long preliminaries of the parade and the seemingly endless time that the horses take to cross Epsom Downs to reach the mile and a half start were over. The start was then delayed for a further nine minutes by the antics of Ribero who refused to go into the stalls. Eventually, the starter lost patience with him and he was withdrawn and took no part in the race.

As expected Hipster made the early running, but the pace was so fast that he had to surrender the lead to Connaught after the first half-mile. From then on Jim Joel's horse strode out in front keeping up a tremendous gallop down the hill to Tattenham Corner with Piggott on Park Top tucked in close behind him. Turning into the straight Connaught held a clear lead over the mare, with Remand and Mount Athos in close attendance. With three furlongs to go, Jim Joel's black jacket and red cap were still in front, but Lester had not moved on Park Top. Remand was the first to weaken and fall away. With two furlongs left Barclay on the rails was riding Connaught for all he was worth. Hutchinson on Mount Athos challenged him on the outside, and behind them Lester, whom the racing correspondent of *Le Figaro* once described as "the man of marble", was still motionless. Time stood still as the two leaders were driven for the line with all the force their riders could command, with Lester like a graven image on their tails. The cheering reached a crescendo but I did not hear a sound. My whole attention was riveted onto Piggott and the mare. At last, with barely a

72

hundred yards left, he gave Park Top her head. She had a beautiful clear run between the two colts and seemed to glide effortlessly through the gap. Once in front Lester asked no more of her. Connaught had dropped back beaten, but for a dreadful moment I thought the master jockey had taken things too easily. Hutchinson had never stopped riding Mount Athos and it looked for a split second as if he would catch us. But Lester had not misjudged events. At the post Park Top had three quarters of a length to spare over Mount Athos, with Connaught a length and a half away third. A further six lengths behind came Remand.

It had been a breathtaking performance. Lester had never gone for his whip, indeed he had hardly moved throughout the race. He had shown complete confidence in the mare's brilliant burst of speed, and she had not let him down. The rest of the day remains a blur of happiness, especially the moment of triumph when Maureen led Park Top and Lester into the winner's unsaddling enclosure, that circle of grass trodden by the hooves of the most famous horses in the history of the Turf. We whose lives for the past two years had become inextricably bound up with her fortunes could savour to the full her presence on the most sought-after piece of turf racing has to offer. For Bernard, it was a magnificent training achievement and a triumph of will and character in defying his illness.

Of course Park Top had not won the Derby, but for me it was as if she had. She had finally proved that she had joined the ranks of the greatest mares and fillies in the history of racing. There followed an interview on television of which all I remember is discussing the colour of my socks which matched my racing silks. Pale yellow socks had become a talisman to bring good fortune to Park Top on the race-course. Since she retired the efficacy of the charm has worn off. Nowadays I wear socks of a more sombre hue when going to see a fancied horse run.

The following morning, *The Sporting Life* carried on its front page a wonderful photograph of Maureen leading in Park Top. The caption read "The return of the champion". It was no less than the truth.

An analysis of the mare's performance showed what a magnificent race she had run. In an earlier chapter I have told of how her time was more than two seconds faster than Blakeney in the Derby and Sleeping Partner in the Oaks. One well-known racing journalist made the point that it was a measure of Park Top's brilliance that she could win a race run in exceptionally fast time without being really extended. The previous year Sir Ivor had beaten Connaught easily by three-quarters of a length, now Park Top had defeated the same horse every bit as easily by two and a quarter lengths in a time that was more than a second faster than Sir Ivor's. On both occasions the going had been good with the strength and direction of the wind marginally favouring Sir Ivor. The average times of the other races run on the day of Sir Ivor's Derby tended to be faster than those run on the day of Park Top's victory. Evidence that Connaught was as good as ever came a fortnight later when he slammed Wolver Hollow by five lengths in the ten-furlong Prince of Wales Stakes at Royal Ascot. With such evidence, it is certainly arguable that Park Top would have beaten Sir Ivor had they met when both were at their best and over a distance of a mile and a half on good going.

When I had returned to earth, it was time to think about Park Top's next race. She had suffered no ill effects after Epsom so Bernard suggested running her in the Hardwicke Stakes at Royal Ascot. This is another mile and a half race for four-year-olds and upwards, second only in prestige to the Coronation Cup. One of the attractions of running at Ascot was that Chicago was likely to be in the field. I was convinced Park Top had not given her true running in the Cumberland Lodge the previous autumn and only another meeting between the two horses could settle the matter. The Hardwicke is run on the Friday of the Royal Meeting, thus Park Top had a fortnight to recover from her Epsom exertions.

My enjoyment of the Royal Meeting was marred by the usual apprehension aroused by the coming clash with Chicago. Winning the Coronation Cup had established Park Top as an outstanding race-horse. From now on it was not a question of trying to reach the top of the tree, but the more difficult task of staying there. Now anything less than victory would be an anticlimax. Those few who still denied she was a great mare, and there were a few, would seize on any future failure as evidence that the Coronation Cup win had been a fluke. After Epsom, Park Top's every race appearance carried with it for her admirers the anxiety that she might fall from her pinnacle.

By the time Ascot took place, the coughing epidemic was beginning to take its toll. Park Top had only three rivals. Chicago, after a disappointing fourth in the Jockey Club Stakes, had shown that he was back to his best by beating the good four-year-old colt Alignment in the two-miles Henry II Stakes at Sandown at the end of May. Alignment had previously won a valuable one mile seven furlongs handicap carrying ten stone. As a three-year-old this colt had won three races, including the Ebor Handicap, so Chicago's Sandown victory was a good performance. The remaining two runners were both four-year-olds. Rangong, by Right Royal out of a Pinza mare and trained by Noel Murless, had been very lightly raced, running once unplaced as a two-year-old and once as a three-year-old when second, beaten a head by Lucky Finish in the Dante Stakes over an extended mile and a quarter at York. The Dante is an established Derby trial. Ribero had finished a short head behind Rangong in third place. Murless's horse came into its own as a four-year-old. He won his first race of the season, the mile and a half Aston Park Stakes at Newbury, beating among others Fortissimo. After Royal Ascot, he was to win the St. Simon Stakes at Newbury, beating the Jockey Club Stakes winner Torpid, and the Geoffrey Freer Stakes over a rather longer distance on the same course. Park Top's old rival of the previous year, Canterbury, was third in the latter race. The fourth runner was the filly Bringley who in her two previous races had finished third to Crozier in the John Porter and had been unplaced in the Yorkshire Cup. To our disappointment Piggott was unable to take the ride on the mare as he had been suspended by the Stewards of the Jockey Club shortly before. The suspension was due to start on the day of the Hardwicke.

As soon as I heard the news, and still being a Steward I was among the first to know, I telephoned Bernard, and we decided to offer the ride to Park Top's old partner Geoff Lewis, who at once accepted. It was fortunate that there was such a small field or Lewis in all probability would not have been available. The main question posed by the race was whether the mare could take her revenge on Chicago, although it was not entirely a two-horse race as Rangong had made many friends when winning at Newbury.

The going was ideal and the sun shone, a good omen for us. The Hardwicke was the fourth race on the card, so I had most of the afternoon to endure before the long-awaited yet dreaded moment of the "off".

As a race, the Hardwicke was a complete contrast to the Coronation Cup. At Epsom it had been a strong gallop from the start, resulting in an exceptionally fast time. Now with Chicago in the lead, the four runners were only cantering for the first half-mile. Park Top was second, followed by Rangong and Bringley in Indian file. It was only after passing the mile post that Hutchinson on Chicago increased the pace. The order remained unchanged until the field turned into the straight. Once in line for home, Hutchinson set about the Harry Wragg-trained colt for all he was worth, making the best of his way home. From the stands I could appreciate what must have been going through Lewis's mind. He must have recalled all too clearly how the previous September he had taken the lead on the mare with more than a furlong to run, only to be caught and left standing by Chicago inside the distance. Now Geoff just sat and suffered behind his old adversary, fearful of losing the race by making his effort too soon. No praise can be too high for the coolness he showed. He waited and waited just as Lester had done a fortnight before. Then, well inside the final furlong he unleashed the mare. Although Chicago was not stopping, Park Top's great speed would not be denied. In a matter of yards she was in front, going on to win hard-held by a length and a half from Chicago. Bringley ran on in the final stages to pass Rangong for third place.

It was an immensely satisfactory victory, for not only had the mare taken her revenge on Chicago, but she had shown herself to be the complete race-horse. She could win in top-class company however the race was run, be it at a cracking gallop from pillar to post as at Epsom, or as here when it had been virtually a sprint over the last few furlongs. Whereas the time at Epsom had been very fast, at Ascot it was outstandingly slow, 22 seconds slower than the average. Since the going was good a fast time would have been expected.

As is often the case in slowly-run races, the jockeys concerned came in for criticism in the press the next day for allowing the race to be run at a false pace. Such criticism is usually unjust since the object of a jockey's tactics is to win. If all the jockeys concerned are of the opinion that they would damage their chances by setting a strong early gallop, it must be right for them to refrain from doing so. When a horse is beaten after making much of the running, one invariably hears the comment that the jockey made too much early use of the horse. In this case, Chicago's connections felt the slowly-run race had been against their horse and when he met the mare again in the King George VI and Queen Elizabeth Stakes Harry Wragg provided a pacemaker.

Park Top's convincing win in the Hardwicke, coupled with the equally emphatic win of Connaught in the Prince of Wales, established the mare as the best horse above the age of three over a distance of ground in the country. As yet, there was no evidence of how she would fare when she met the top three-year-olds.

The first two opportunities for this were the Eclipse Stakes over a mile and a quarter at Sandown three weeks after Royal Ascot, and the King George VI and Queen Elizabeth Stakes over a mile and a half at Ascot at the end of July. As the mare had now had three races in a month, she was entitled to a rest. Accordingly, we decided to give her an easy, and make the King George VI and Queen Elizabeth Stakes her next objective. The coughing epidemic was growing worse every day. Hardly a stable in the country remained unaffected. There was even talk of suspending racing altogether until the epidemic abated. Stanley House had not escaped but Park Top did, perhaps because of the severe attack of equine 'flu she suffered as a two-year-old. It was about this time that Bernard went into hospital for his operation. However, in no time, he was conducting his stable affairs from his bed. He was also fully acquainted with what was happening in the racing world and in particular how the coughing epidemic was affecting the likely line-up for the Eclipse.

The famous Sandown race was due to be run on July 5th. In the weeks prior to the race it was generally thought that it would be largely a two-horse race between Connaught, a better horse over a mile and a quarter than a mile and a half, and the brilliant miler Right Tack. This colt, by Hard Tack, was trained by John Sutcliffe at Epsom. As a two-year-old he had won five of his six starts. His first three victories were modest affairs, but the horse finished the season in brilliant fashion winning the Imperial Stakes at Kempton, worth more than £7,000, and the Middle Park Stakes at Newmarket. With the possible exception of the Observer Gold Cup, the Middle Park is the most coveted two-year-old prize for colts in the season. Provided he is engaged in them its winner always features prominently in the winter betting for the following season's Two Thousand Guineas and Derby. As a three-year-old the colt went from strength to strength. Although defeated in his first outing by Tower Walk in the Greenham Stakes at Newbury, where he was giving the winner weight, he went on to win the Two Thousand Guineas comfortably, reversing the positions with Tower Walk whom he beat by two and a half lengths. Right Tack was then sent to the Curragh for the Irish Two Thousand Guineas, which he also won. His next race was the St. James's Palace Stakes at Royal Ascot, a race by tradition the target of the Two Thousand Guineas winner as it is also over a mile. Starting a six to four against favourite, he beat a top class field of five. Habitat, the recent winner of the Lockinge Stakes at Newbury, was second. This horse was to be unbeaten in his remaining races of the season, which included the Wills mile and the Prix du Moulin at Longchamp. Right Tack had been ridden by Lewis in all his races except for the first two, and he had been booked to ride the Epsom-trained colt in the Eclipse.

Although Park Top had been left in the Eclipse, it was not the intention to run her. Since a mile and a half was the mare's best distance it seemed to be asking too much of her to take on a brilliant miler like Right Tack, to say nothing of Connaught over his best distance. The coughing epidemic was now at its height. A week before the race Right Tack fell a victim, leaving Lewis without a ride. I was over in Ireland staying with friends for the Irish Derby, run a week before the Sandown race. The first I knew of Right Tack's withdrawal was when Bernard rang me up on the Friday night with the news. As a result, Bernard now wanted to run the mare. Although she was not fully tuned up Bernard was confident he could get her ready in time for the race, provided she had a strong gallop on the following Tuesday. A decision had to be made quickly.

There was, in addition, the problem of who would be available to ride. I was rather against running as I felt the distance was too short for us. At first Bernard accepted this, but later the same night he telephoned again, urging me to reconsider my decision. This time, he persuaded me to let the mare take her chance. The question of her jockey could be decided after the weekend. As so often before a big race, those with runners had to wait on Lester to make up his mind as to which horse he would ride. Among those he was considering for the Eclipse was Ribofilio, trained by Fulke Johnson Houghton and owned by Charlie Engelhard. The colt, to be ridden by Piggott, was favourite for the next day's Irish Derby, and it would not be until after it had been run that Lester would make up his mind. Ribofilio had been given top weight in the two-year-old Free Handicap for the previous year as a result of his victory in the Champagne Stakes at Doncaster and the Dewhurst Stakes at Newmarket. He had won his opening race of the current season, the Ascot Two Thousand Guineas Trial, but in the Two Thousand Guineas itself, after starting favourite at 15-8, he had run a lifeless race, being virtually pulled up with a quarter of a mile still to run. In spite of this the colt had started 7-2 favourite in Blakeney's Derby. Here he ran better than at Newmarket, finishing fifth, beaten about three and a half lengths by the winner. Although he was taking on horses in the Irish Derby that had finished in front of him at Epsom, he was still favourite for the Curragh classic, simply because he would be ridden by Piggott.

Aware that on the running of Ribofilio in the Irish Derby would depend whether Lester would be free to take the mount on Park Top in the Eclipse, the race held special interest for me. Ribofilio looked all over the winner at the distance, but Prince Regent, third in the Epsom Derby, came with a late run to beat him by a length.

I returned to London on the Monday; in the evening I went to see Bernard in hospital. I was delighted to find him up and dressed. He was busy making entries and dealing with the other office aspects of a trainer's life. Disregarding everything he had been told by his doctor, Bernard told me he was going to drive down to Newmarket the following morning to supervise Park Top's final gallop before the Eclipse. He asked me to go with him. I had had a strenuous weekend in Ireland, and having caught an early aeroplane that morning was planning a lie-in the following day. To see Park Top do her final gallop would mean leaving London at 5.30 a.m. so I refused. I then decided that if Bernard, still recovering from a major operation, could get up then I, with nothing worse than a hangover, could do the same. I shall always be grateful to Bernard for taking me to Newmarket that early July morning. It has remained in my memory as one of the happiest interludes in Park Top's racing career.

Watching early morning work on Newmarket Heath is one of the greatest joys of being involved in racing. The quiet and the peace is in complete contrast to the noisy hurly-burly of the race-course. The only sounds are the larks and thudding hooves. This particular morning was as lovely as an English summer can produce. The mare was to work over a mile on the Limekilns, the famous summer gallop on the Bury side of the town. After walking and trotting round the paddock adjoining the stables the horses went by a back route to the Heath, while Bernard and I drove the short distance. Once on the Limekilns, Maureen got off Park Top and handed her over to George Douglas, one of Bernard's chief work riders. Maureen always rode the mare when she had cantering exercise, but Bernard would put George or Frank Morby on her for fast work because of their extra strength.

The procedure followed in these gallops was always the same. The lead horse, in this case Shaft, no mean performer himself and another of Lester's winners on Arc de Triomphe day, would set off in front at a good gallop, with Park Top three to four lengths behind. Then with about a furlong and a half to go, the mare would be given her head. This was the critical moment. If she was to satisfy Bernard, she would have to close the gap in a few strides and then take the lead. Park Top galloped at home as brilliantly and consistently as she did on the race-course. That morning was to be no exception. The moment George asked her she lengthened her stride and was at once upsides and then in front of Shaft. At the end of the mile she was clear and being held on a tight rein. The mare was then handed back to Maureen, who had been watching the gallop with all the anxiety of a proud father watching his son go in to bat at a critical moment in a key inter-school cricket match. Bernard and I then went back to breakfast at Northmore feeling well content with what we'd seen.

On returning to London we learnt that Ribofilio's connections had decided to run him in the Eclipse and that Lester was to ride. The colt would be a formidable rival but I took comfort in the fact that he had had a very hard race at the Curragh and that the two races came very close together. The jockey problem was now settled for us. Lewis was the obvious choice and he accepted the ride.

The next turn of events was the news that Connaught was

the latest victim of the cough and would not run. Noel Murless, however, still had two strings to his bow, the three-year-old Hill Run and the year older Timmy My Boy. The former was bred in America and unbeaten in his only two starts. As a two-year-old he won the important Hyperion Stakes over six furlongs at the Ascot Heath July meeting. In the current season he had won the Prix Jean Prat over nine furlongs at Chantilly. This race, though not of outstanding value by French standards, carried with it considerable prestige. Timmy My Boy had been trained in France as a two- and three-year-old. In his first season his best performance was running third to Sir Ivor in the Grand Criterion over a mile at Longchamp. This was good form as the race is the most important two-year-old event in France. In his second season this Tantième colt had run six times, winning the Prix Eugène Adam over a mile and a half at Saint-Cloud. This was an outstanding performance, since he beat Zeddaan, who had previously won the French Two Thousand Guineas. Since going to Noel Murless at Newmarket Timmy My Boy had run once, finishing second to Grandier in the mile and three furlongs Prix d'Harcourt, another highly prized race in France. His showing in the race was evidence that Timmy My Boy was as good a four-year-old as he had been at three, since Grandier in his previous race had finished second to Carmarthen, a very good French horse, in the £28,000 Prix Ganay. To show just how good the form was, Grandier had been placed only two pounds below Vaguely Noble and one below Sir Ivor in the previous season's French Free Handicap for three-year-olds and upwards. Timmy My Boy himself had been rated fourth best three-year-old with eight stone thirteen pounds, the same weight as had been given to Park Top.

No sooner had Murless decided to run Hill Run in the Eclipse and Timmy My Boy in the Grand Prix de St. Cloud than the former got the cough. Timmy My Boy was then switched to the

Sandown race. At the same time came the news that Ribofilio was also a non-runner for the same reason. The absence of Charlie Engelhard's horse greatly reduced the significance of the Eclipse, since it meant that there would not be a top-class three-year-old in the field. It also meant that Lester was left without a ride.

Bernard and I discussed standing Geoff Lewis down in favour of Lester. We both agreed that this would be wrong. Lewis had accepted our firm offer. Had he not done so, he would almost certainly by now have obtained another ride. Furthermore he had ridden a brilliant race on the mare in the Hardwicke. It is true that had Piggott been available when we first decided to run he would have got the mount. Equally, had Right Tack not fallen a victim to the cough Park Top would not have been in the field herself. As in other spheres of life, racing is made up of ifs and buts.

By the day of the race, the field had been reduced to seven. The only three-year-old was Rocked, trained in Ireland by Seamus McGrath. The colt had won his last race, the French Fir Stakes, over a mile on the Curragh. Previously he had finished seventh in the Newmarket Two Thousand Guineas and the form did not look good enough for him to pose a serious threat. Of the four-year-olds, Remand and Hogarth looked the most dangerous. The latter was an Italian horse who had won that country's Derby the previous year. Over from France was another four-year-old, Lightwind, whose best performance to date had been to win a moderate £3,000 event over a mile at Maisons Laffitte the previous October. The remaining four-year-old in the line up was Royal Rocket. In his only previous run of the season he had finished third to Connaught in the Coronation Stakes over the same course and distance as the Eclipse. This had been back in April. The remaining runner was the five-year-old Wolver Hollow. In his previous three seasons he had run sixteen times, winning twice over ten furlongs and once over a mile. As a two-year-old he had failed to win in four starts. It was only at his fifth attempt as a three-year-old that he succeeded in being first past the post. This was in the Virginia Stakes for three- and four-year-olds over rather more than a mile and three furlongs at Newcastle. Like Park Top and Right Tack, Wolver Hollow's history was to be one of rags to riches. Following another victory in the equally modest Crathorne Stakes over the York mile in September, he did not win again. However his final run of the year saw by far his best performance. He finished third, carrying eight stone one, in the Cambridgeshire. The following season, as a four-year-old, although he won only once from four starts, he never ran a bad race. He did not appear until August by which time he must have impressed his trainer, for he was sent over to Deauville. There he had two races, the first being the £11,000 Prix Gontaut-Biron for four-year-olds and upwards over a mile and a quarter. Wolver Hollow finished a respectable fourth to the previously unbeaten Frontal. Ten days later he reappeared in the £5,000 Prix Ridgeway over the same distance. This time he beat Right Honourable by half a length. I have already discussed the significance of this race. Back in England, Wolver Hollow ran second to World Cup in the Queen Elizabeth II Stakes over the old mile at Ascot. World Cup was a three-year-old who had won the seven furlong Jersey Stakes at Royal Ascot and had then finished second, conceding one pound, to Petingo in the £12,000 Sussex Stakes at Goodwood. This was good form. Petingo was to be placed third in the three-year-old Free Handicap at the end of the season, five pounds below Sir Ivor, and three pounds less than Ribero. In the Queen Elizabeth II Stakes, Wolver Hollow was meeting World Cup at only one pound worse than weight-for-age. For his last race of the year, the colt again challenged for the Cambridgeshire. He ran an even better race than the previous year, finishing second, beaten a neck by Emerilo to whom he was giving twenty-seven pounds.

On his 1968 Cambridgeshire running Wolver Hollow was entitled to be treated with respect in any company in races of a mile to a mile and a quarter. From the way he ran in his early races as a five-year-old, it would appear that the horse did not always give his best. His first race was in the Kempton Park Jubilee Handicap, by tradition one of the most competitive middle distance handicaps in the early weeks of the season. Due to his Cambridgeshire running he had been set to carry top weight of nine stone seven. As in the previous year's Cambridgeshire he finished second, giving thirty-five pounds to the winner Sovereign Ruler, who, in his previous race, had been narrowly beaten by Karabas (another of the stars in Bernard's stable) in Epsom's City and Suburban. Although Wolver Hollow was beaten eight lengths this was a fine performance, as there were good horses including Karabas behind him. There followed a disappointing run when he finished last in Newbury's Lockinge Stakes for which he was well backed. As we have seen, in his following race he was trounced by Connaught at Royal Ascot.

From his running in these last two races, it seemed reasonable to conclude that when running in handicaps Wolver Hollow was very much a horse to be reckoned with, but was no match for top class horses at weight-for-age. Lester was offered and accepted the ride.

The going for the Eclipse was firm which did not worry us. The fact, however, that on all known form Park Top ought to win made the hours leading up to it all the more agonizing.

She started 5-4 on favourite, with Timmy My Boy at 13-2, and Wolver Hollow 8-1, being backed down from 100-8. Considering he had been sent from Italy, Hogarth was at the rather surprising odds of 33-1.

The steady reduction in the number of runners continued until the very last moment. While walking round immediately before entering his stall, the luckless Remand lashed out and hit the framework. This caused him to go lame. The starter was in a difficult position. He could not allow the horse to take part while lame, at the same time there was no way of telling how seriously Remand had injured himself. Understandably, he decided to withdraw Jakie's colt, so only seven horses took part in the race. It was cruel luck on Remand as he was greatly fancied that afternoon. It turned out that the lameness was only of very brief duration and he returned to the paddock sound.

From Park Top's point of view the Eclipse was a tragedy. The Sandown mile and a quarter is a difficult course to ride even for the most experienced jockey. There is a long right-handed bend into the straight, and the final two furlongs are uphill which makes it essential to be well placed early in the straight. It is all too easy to get shut in during the turn for home. Bernard had told Lewis to keep clear of the rails rounding the bend to avoid such a situation. Rocked made the early running from Hogarth and Royal Rocket, with Park Top fifth and Wolver Hollow last. The order remained the same as they swung into the turn. To my dismay, I saw through my glasses Lewis had Park Top tucked in behind the leaders on the rails, and not on the outside as had been planned. As the horses straightened up for home with rather more than two furlongs to run, Hogarth challenged Rocked on the latter's outside while at the same time Barclay made his move on Timmy My Boy on the outside of Hogarth. At the two-furlong pole, Lewis on Park Top found himself behind a wall of three horses. Both for him and for Park Top's supporters on the stands it was a dreadful moment. Lewis had to take a split-second decision; should he take a chance that the pacemaker Rocked would weaken and veer away from the rails as a tired horse often does, thus giving him an opening, or should he check the mare and take her to the outside? He decided on a compromise and tried to find an opening between Hogarth and Timmy My Boy.

This move proved unavailing as no gap opened up between them. Park Top then had to be checked again and brought to the outside of Timmy My Boy before she could finally deliver her challenge. In the meantime no sooner had Park Top moved away from the rails than Piggott on Wolver Hollow took her place. A few strides later, Rocked did hang away to the left giving Lester the opening he needed. In a flash, he drove Wolver Hollow through the gap and into the lead. Then, with all his inimitable strength he set off for the winning post. Poor Geoff had lost lengths in his manoeuvres to find an opening and by the time the mare could make her run on the outside the race was over, safe in the grasp of Piggott and Wolver Hollow. Park Top flew past Hogarth and Timmy My Boy, but Wolver Hollow was gone beyond recall. In the last fifty yards Park Top's brilliant speed had spent itself, and she was no longer closing the gap on the winner.

It had been a traumatic experience watching the closing stages of the race. The whole drama took about half a minute, but it seemed a lifetime. If Geoff Lewis should ever read these lines, I hope he will forgive me if I say I think his riding of the mare was at fault that afternoon. At the same time, one must remember he had had to make a difficult decision in less time than it takes either to write or read these words. I was watching the race with Debo and as Park Top passed the post she turned and gave me the best possible advice. She said: "Don't say anything." Walking to the unsaddling enclosure, we were joined by Bernard. By tacit agreement we found it luckier to watch Park Top's races apart. None of us spoke. Lewis rode the mare to the place reserved for second, took the saddle off and went into the weighing room in total silence. Some time afterwards, talking to Bernard on a flight back from Paris, Geoff was generous enough to tell him that after the finish of the Eclipse he prayed for the earth to open up and swallow him. The only wry satisfaction Bernard and I got from the result was the delighted reaction of Wolver Hollow's former trainer to the horse's triumph over the mighty Park Top. A month earlier at Epsom, we had been riled to hear Cecil Boyd-Rochfort remarking to all and sundry how he could not understand running a horse like Park Top in a race of the class of the Coronation Cup. "What is a mare like that doing in this field?" he could be heard saying in the Paddock. Now he was bursting with pride at Wolver Hollow's triumph over the mare.

While Park Top's defeat was a bitter disappointment I was far from dejected. She had been a most gallant loser against impossible odds, giving her all. Her reputation suffered in no way in defeat. She could still hold her proud head high.

*   *   *

One of the blessings of ownership is that provided a horse remains sound and well, no sooner is one race over than plans can be laid for the next. Park Top showed no ill effects from her gallant if unavailing efforts in the Eclipse. Her programme therefore remained unchanged, with the King George VI and Queen Elizabeth Stakes, to be run on July 26th at Ascot, as her next objective. The Ascot race is the most important mile-and-a-half event for three-year-olds and upwards of the English flat racing season. It is our equivalent to the Prix de l'Arc de Triomphe in France. Largely due to the fact that the Longchamp race carries far more prize money, the King George VI and Queen Elizabeth Stakes does not carry the same prestige as the Arc. This is a great pity since the King George VI and Queen Elizabeth Stakes comes at a far better time of year for the supreme test of horseracing, the English race being run in high summer while the Arc takes place so late in the year that many of the contestants are past their best. In 1969, the winner of the Ascot race received £31,000 while the horse that took the Arc earned nearly £89,000, the prize money for the second horse being equivalent to the winning stake in the King George VI and Queen Elizabeth Stakes. In recent years, thanks to the sponsorship of the race by De Beers, the King George VI and Queen Elizabeth Stakes prize money has come more in line with that of the Arc.

The coughing epidemic continued unabated. Bernard's stable was as badly affected as any, but Park Top still remained free from infection. All the same, the weeks between the Eclipse and Ascot were an anxious time. Whenever the telephone rang my first thought was that it would be Bernard ringing up to say Park Top had fallen a victim. In fact she went from strength to strength during this time. Between Sandown and Ascot her performance in one particular gallop showed her brilliant speed. One morning she was working over a mile on the Lime-kilns with George Douglas again in the saddle. Bernard had some Americans staying with him and they accompanied him to watch the gallop. In America race horses do their fast work on the race track where all their serious training is carried out. American trainers and racing enthusiasts attach great impor-tance to the time taken by a horse in training gallops. The horses are timed by stop watch not only over the full distance of the gallop but over each furlong separately. Bernard's guests had arrived on the Limekilns armed with their stop watches and were able to follow their practice by timing Park Top over the last part of her gallop since each furlong is marked by a fir branch stuck into the ground. Douglas was quite unaware that the mare's gallop would be timed and he followed the standard pattern of such work. The mare set off well behind the lead horse, only closing up and passing the latter in the last furlong and a half. The Limekilns are renowned for being a stiff gallop, the ground being slightly uphill throughout. On this occasion everything went as usual, with Park Top getting into top gear in the last quarter of a mile and drawing up to the lead horse in effortless style and then going right away. As he was pulling up Douglas noticed that the American visitors were running towards him, clearly in a state of some excitement. His first reaction was that something must be wrong, although nothing appeared to be amiss.

His anxiety was put at rest when the breathless watchers caught up with him. Between gasps they told him that the mare had covered the last furlong in 11 seconds. Such a time was indeed something to be excited about. As I have already said, for a horse to cover a furlong during a middle distance race in 12 seconds is good going. Indeed the average time of the Epsom five furlongs course, an exceptionally fast track, is 57 seconds, while at Goodwood, another speedy five furlong course, it is 60 seconds, an average time of 12 seconds per furlong. Yet on this particular morning, in a routine one mile gallop accompanied by only one moderate horse, Park Top had done the last furlong in 11 seconds, a time rarely achieved in top class sprint racers let alone over a distance of a mile.

Many years ago the late Edgar Wallace, a keen racing man, wrote a novel called *The Flying Fifty-Five*, about a legendary horse that covered five furlongs in 55 seconds. That particular July morning on Newmarket Heath Park Top showed the same legendary speed at the end of her gallop. When told what had happened, I was yet again reminded of the electric burst of speed she had shown as a yearliing which had so astonished her breeder, Mrs. Scott.

As the day for the King George VI and Queen Elizabeth Stakes approached, it became clear that, like the Eclipse, the field would be a sub-standard one. In particular there would be no three-year-olds taking part, so once again Park Top had no chance to show her ability against the winners of the year's classic races. This meant that there would be no problem in making a firm arrangement with Piggott to ride the mare.

The race eventually attracted a field of nine. There was one eight-year-old, a moderate horse named Coolroy whom Gerry Oldham had leased to act as pacemaker for Chicago, thus ensuring there would be no repetition of the slowly-run Hardwicke Stakes six weeks before. There were two six-year-olds, Crozier who had run second in the mile and a half Grand Prix de Lyon in his only run since finishing fifth in the Coronation Cup, and the Japanese-owned Speed Symboli. This horse, by Royal Challenger out of a Rising Light mare, had as a four-year-old won four top-class races in Japan and then had shown up well when finishing fifth in the Washington International. He had kept his form as a five-year-old, winning three good races in his own country. Now at six, before being sent to be trained in France, he had won two further races in Japan. It was difficult to weigh up his chance but in appearance he looked a little outclassed. The five-year-old Chicago had made an unavailing journey to France to finish unplaced in the Grand Prix de Saint-Cloud after his defeat in the Hardwicke. Of the four four-year-olds, Hogarth from Italy and Timmy My Boy had finished third and fourth behind Wolver Hollow and Park Top in the Eclipse and neither had had a race since Sandown. The other two were both trained in France. Soyeux in his last run had finished third in the Grand Prix de St. Cloud. He was an unlucky horse, constantly running well in the highest class, and finishing fourth in both the French Derby and St. Leger in the previous year. In the latter race he was beaten by a neck by Levmoss for third place. Finally there was Felicio II who appeared to represent the chief danger to the mare. In his last outing he had won the

£58,000 Grand Prix de Saint-Cloud, beating the French Derby winner Goodley by a head. Previous to this he had won the valuable Prix Jean de Chaudenay, also at Saint-Cloud. As a three-year-old, Felicio's best performance was to run Royal Palace to half a length in the King George VI and Queen Elizabeth Stakes.

This form was not as good as it sounds, since Royal Palace broke down in the closing stages of the race and pulled up lame. Nevertheless, he had showed himself a very good horse that day since Ribero, Sir Ivor's conqueror in the Irish Sweeps Derby, was more than five lengths behind him.

The day of the race was hot and sunny. Superstitious as always, I did not want to wear the same brown felt hat as I had donned for the Eclipse. I could not very well wear the top hat that had witnessed the mare's Coronation Cup triumph. In the end I settled for a straw hat and hoped for the best.

The going was firm. This was in our favour, although ideally I think Bernard would have liked just a little more give in the ground. Debo and I drove down from London, both feeling sick with apprehension. Apart from the fact that the mare was racing for the richest prize that she had yet competed for, there were a number of questions to be answered. The unlucky defeat at Sandown entailed her having an unsuccessful but very hard race which might have soured her outlook on racing. Would Chicago having a pace-maker enable him to reverse the Hardwicke running and confirm his defeat of the mare in the previous year's Cumberland Lodge? How good was the previously unraced-in-Europe Speed Symboli, and, most vital of all, could we beat Felicio II, the recent conqueror of the French Derby winner, and a close second in the previous year's running of this Ascot all-aged classic?

If she was to maintain the reputation she had established

by winning the Coronation Cup, and which her defeat in the Eclipse had not affected, then Park Top must win, Felicio or no Felicio.

Bernard was his usual calm, reassuring self and the mare looked magnificent, better perhaps than ever before. I was not alone in thinking this; Alec Marsh, the starter at Ascot on that great day, told me at the Doncaster Leger meeting of 1975 that in his view Park Top's appearance before the start of the King George VI and Queen Elizabeth Stakes epitomised what a really great race-horse should look like on the day of her greatest challenge.

At luncheon before the race, Debo had the good fortune to sit next to Bing Crosby, a keen race-goer, which gave her something to take her mind off the race. I do not remember who had the misfortune to be my neighbours. I was silent and preoccupied and my diet more liquid than solid. Eventually the time came for Bernard to saddle the mare, and Lester joined us in the paddock and moments later Bernard was giving him a leg up and the waiting was over.

Park Top strode out beautifully on her way to the start of the now familiar triangular-shaped mile and a half course at Ascot. She had opened in the ring at 7-4 with Felicio at 11-4. Timmy My Boy was next best at 6-1 and Chicago 8-1. Park Top weakened a little while Felicio strengthened in the market and at the off they were joint favourites at 9-4.

The sun was shining on Lester's straw silks as it had shone on them on the day of the Ribblesdale rather more than two years before. I could only hope and pray history would repeat itself.

Debo and I stationed ourselves at the top and back of the stand next to a doorway so that we could escape quickly after the race. Quickly, to avoid having to put a good face on defeat in front of friends and even more quickly if the miracle happened and Maureen would lead her into the winner's enclosure.

Park Top was the last to enter the stalls and a few seconds later they were on their way. As expected Greville Starkey took Coolroy to the front setting a strong gallop down the hill to Swinley Bottom. He was followed by Speed Symboli and Timmy My Boy with Hogarth close behind, then Chicago and Soyeux. Felicio was last but one with only Park Top behind him. The order remained virtually unchanged as they passed the mile post and swung right-handed up the hill. Bill Pyers on Felicio knew his horse had to come from behind while Lester was equally determined to ride a waiting race on Park Top.

From the start until the turn into the straight the two horses remained at the rear of the field, alternating between last and last but one. At the head of affairs, Coolroy continued in front admirably fulfilling his role of pacemaker. With about half a mile to go, Felicio repassed Park Top and although the angle of Lester's behind still gave cause for confidence, I was getting anxious. The mare had all of ten lengths to make up on the leaders and it is usually essential to be well placed at the turn into the straight when there are only three furlongs left to run. Indeed, as they swung right-handed for the last time Park Top was still last and I momentarily lost faith, turning to Debo muttering "Not today".

As I spoke the words, a transformation came over the race. The bell rang and the nine runners were in the straight. Coolroy was still just in front but Speed Symboli quickly drew level and then passed him. Timmy My Boy on the outside of the Japanese colt was almost upsides the leaders with Hogarth just behind, and followed by Crozier and Chicago. Soyeux ran a little wide coming into the straight carrying Pyers on Felicio with him just as the latter was starting his run on the outside of the field. Piggott also made a forward move on the turn but kept the mare to the inside. With just over two furlongs to go

Speed Symboli was in front with Coolroy weakening rapidly on the rails. Crozier took over with about a furlong and a half left to run, while both Hogarth and Felicio had every chance if they were good enough. Meanwhile Piggott found an opening between Coolroy on the rails and Speed Symboli. He was through it and past Crozier in a few strides and with more than a furlong left to run the race was to all intents and purposes over. In many ways the race resembled the Twyford Stakes at Newbury in 1967, in that Park Top went from last to first in less than a furlong, the difference being of course that in the Newbury race she was taking on second-class fillies whereas now she was opposed by some of the best middle-distance colts in Europe. As soon as Piggott asked her to go she just swept the opposition aside in a matter of moments. Crozier, probably running the best race of his long and honourable career, ran on gamely and finished second, beaten one and a half lengths, with Hogarth a length further away. Then came Felicio another three lengths back.

After the race Felicio's connections claimed that he had been bumped by Soyeux early in the straight, after which he lost interest in the contest. This may well be true, although he finished further in front of the latter than he had done when winning at St. Cloud three weeks earlier.

Chicago ran a most disappointing race finishing last except for his pacemaker. Although Hogarth finished closer to the mare than in the Eclipse, Park Top's winning margin is misleading. Unless you had seen the race or a film of it the mare's superiority to her rivals that afternoon is hard to imagine. She completely outclassed them and although it was not a brilliant field, I doubt whether there was a horse in Europe who would haves defeated Park Top on her running that afternoon. Her time of 2 minutes 32.46 seconds was fast, being 4.54 seconds faster than the average time for Ascot's mile and a half. The

THE POETRY OF PARK TOP AND PIGGOTT

Lester Piggott and Park Top gave me one of my most exciting moments on the turf when winning the King George VI and Queen Elizabeth Stakes at Ascot on Saturday, writes Airborne.

From a seemingly hopeless position at the rear of the field, Lester brought his beautiful mount winging up the rail as though nothing else existed in the race.

MATTER OF STRIDES

In a matter of strides he was on the heels of the leaders, and with a furlong still to go, Park Top struck the front, and from then on never seemed in danger of defeat.

Discussing the race afterwards with my wife, she said "It was just like poetry". I couldn't have agreed more; poetry indeed it was.

Those who think that horse racing is concerned only with gambling, should have been at Ascot to see the speed, courage, and beauty of Park Top, and the artistry of the man on her back.

---

previous year, in slightly slower conditions, Royal Palace took three-quarters of a second longer while the winning time on good going in 1967 was even slower. In 1970 Nijinsky won in comparatively slow time, considering the conditions, taking 2 minutes 36.16 seconds. This is probably misleading as he won so easily. All these times have since been surpassed by Grundy in his epic victory over Bustino in the 1975 running of the race.

Piggott took a chance, as it turned out successful, by keeping the mare on the inside. No doubt he reckoned that as on Wolver Hollow in the Eclipse, he would find an opening on the rails as the leader weakened. Indeed he rode almost identical races in the Eclipse and King George VI and Queen Elizabeth Stakes.

As Park Top passed the post, ears pricked and Lester easing her up, Debo and I, from our vantage point by the door, tore down the stairs, only to run into my elder daughter who, arriving late, was charging up them just too late to see the finish. Together we found our way past the entrance to the Royal Box to the winner's unsaddling enclosure. We got there before Bernard, and when he arrived, apparently unmoved, I did not risk speaking for fear of tears. Instead, I contented myself with throwing an arm round his shoulder. It was a moment of supreme happiness, a victory that six months before had seemed, if considered at all, a pipe dream beyond hope of realisation. Maureen led the mare in to a tremendous reception. Indeed it was only when watching the film afterwards that I realised just how great the cheering had been from the moment half way up the straight when it was clear the mare was going to win.

It is no good pretending that I can remember what Lester said on dismounting, nor what I said to the many kind people who crowded round offering their congratulations. My friends knew what winning the race meant to me; but they and that Ascot crowd as well as the millions watching on television knew something far more important. They knew they had seen one of the great race mares of all time. A true champion, as courageous as she was beautiful, with flying hooves the mighty Tetrach would not have scorned.

I remember trying to be polite and correct to Monsieur Boussac when he offered his congratulations as senior steward of

French racing and not making much of a fist of it. Then came an invitation to Debo and myself to receive the Cup from Her Majesty in the Royal Box. It would have been better if I had had a greater sense of reality since my only response to the Queen as she handed me the trophy was to exclaim "Goodness Ma'am – it's heavy", which indeed it was. Her Majesty replied with just a hint of asperity "Of course it is – it's real". As usual, the Queen had missed nothing in the race and commented on the brilliant race Piggott had ridden by keeping her to the inside. Her Majesty's next action was to send her Representative for a bottle of champagne. My mind went back to that other triumphant Ascot day when the mare had won the Ribblesdale, and the rueful look Bernard Norfolk had given to the accumulated empty champagne bottles surrounding Bernard, myself and our friends. Now he returned in next to no time with a full bottle, and the seal of one of the great days of my life was set by the Queen and the Queen Mother drinking a toast to Park Top.

It was then that the Queen Mother said something which I have never forgotten. It could only have been said by someone who really loves racing and race-horses and who understood the emotion involved in owning a great horse. Her Majesty said: "A victory like yours today is something you will have to keep and treasure all your life – it will always be with you." That is true, and Park Top's victory that day has been with me ever since. It is vividly with me now as I write, so that I can see the closing stages of the race as if it were yesterday. Nor will I ever forget the debt of gratitude I owe to Lester for his masterly riding, to Maureen for all the love and care she lavished on Park Top from her earliest days, to George Douglas, Michael Ryan and everyone else at Stanley House. However, as in other fields, it is the leader of the team to whom the greatest credit must go, and therefore my greatest debt is to Bernard van Cutsem, without whose genius as a trainer Park Top's name would never have joined the list of racing immortals.

In case readers should feel I am a prejudiced judge of the mare's ability, my opinion is shared by the man who really is in a position to know – Lester Piggott. In reply to a note I had written to him after Ascot, he wrote: "The mare is the best of her sex I have ever ridden." This letter is among my most treasured possessions. My generation of race-goers will appreciate just how high a tribute Lester was paying the mare, since ten years before he had ridden Petite Etoile to victory in the 1,000 Guineas and the Oaks, triumphs which were followed by many other outstanding victories including two successive Coronation Cups in 1960 and 1961. Until the arrival on the scene of those two wonder mares Dahlia and Allez France, many people would consider Petite Etoile as the greatest race mare since the war.

As his letter shows, Lester thought differently. How my mare compares with the two French mares is anyone's guess. Since she had tremendous speed and stayed every yard of the mile and a half, no matter how fast a race was run, I will only say she would have taxed their abilities to the utmost.

The victory at Ascot settled the problem of Park Top's programme for the remainder of the season. She had established her right to challenge for the greatest race in Europe, the Prix de l'Arc de Triomphe, due to be run at Longchamp on October 5th. For the present she had more than earned a rest. Bernard would then give her one race prior to the great day.

During the first half of August we discussed which race this should be. The final choice lay between the Cumberland Lodge in England and the Prix Foy in France. This latter race run at Longchamp is a recognised trial for the Arc, though its distance is a furlong less. The Ascot race was due to be run on Septem-

"FLORIZEL"

25 THE AVENUE,

NEWMARKET,

SUFFOLK.

July 30ᵗ 1961

Your Grace.

Very many thanks for your kind letter.

For me personally it was a great thrill to win for you on "Park Top," on Saturday.

She is a great mare; and the best of her sex I have ever ridden.

Kindest Regards

Yours Sincerely

Lester

ber 25th while the Longchamp event took place eighteen days earlier on September 7th.

We decided to go for the Prix Foy. Three factors influenced the decision. First, the Cumberland Lodge was only ten days before the Arc and should the mare have a hard race in it there would be little time for her to recover, particularly as Bernard wanted to send her to France at least two clear days before the Arc. Secondly, after her emphatic defeat in the Ascot race the previous year I was prejudiced against it. Finally, there was the matter of prize money. The Foy was worth over £7,500, well over twice the value of the English event.

Park Top did make one public appearance between winning the King George VI and Queen Elizabeth Stakes and her visit to Longchamp on September 7th. This was not on a race-course but at our local Agricultural Show held at Bakewell, three miles from Chatsworth. This show prides itself as being the leading one-day show in the country, putting on the highest class of centre ring entertainment. After her Ascot triumph those organising the show asked me if I would allow the mare to parade round the show ring during the afternoon as an added attraction. I asked Bernard and slightly to my surprise he agreed to the idea. She travelled to Chatsworth in a style befitting her position. Maureen was naturally in attendance, as was the travelling head lad together with a lad for the other horse sent with her as a companion. An apprentice who was to ride the mare round the show ring completed the party. Thus, including the horse-box driver, her entourage numbered five.

Bernard came up from Newmarket to supervise the arrangements at the show. It was the first time for more than thirty years that the stables at Chatsworth had been used and never before had they housed thoroughbreds. Thus it was more than 200 years before James Pain, the architect of the stable block, had inmates worthy of his splendid building. I felt I should put a plaque over the mare's box with the words "Park Top slept here" followed by the dates.

Her appearance was a great success. She was much admired as she was led round with the apprentice wearing a set of my racing silks, while I gave a commentary on her achievements and read out a telegram from Lester wishing her good luck in the show jumping! She seemed fully aware of the admiration she was evoking and showed herself off magnificently. On leaving the ring she passed a hackney stallion and the excited noises she emitted at seeing him seemed to bode well for her stud career.

The rest of August passed uneventfully and by September 1st Park Top's rivals for the Prix Foy began to be announced. Chief among them was Felicio, no doubt his connections were convinced that the bump he received from Soyeux at a critical moment in the King George VI and Queen Elizabeth Stakes had robbed him of his chance and were now anxious to take their revenge. There was another five-year-old, an old rival from the d'Hedouville, Bagdad who in his two previous runs of the season had finished fourth, in the Grand Prix de Saint-Cloud and the Prix d'Harcourt over the same course and distance as the Foy. Since Felicio had won the Saint-Cloud race and Timmy My Boy had finished second in the Harcourt two lengths ahead of Bagdad, the mare seemed to have him well held on her running with Felicio at Ascot. The remaining three runners were all four-year-olds. The mare Pandora Bay had had only one run since finishing second to Park Top in the Prix de la Seine back in May. This was in a valuable mile and a quarter race for mares and fillies at Saint-Cloud in the middle of June. She could only finish fifth of the seven runners so she too appeared to be no great danger to our mare. The same could be said of the colt Danoso whose first appearance of the year it was. In the previous season he had run unplaced in the Arc de Triomphe and in the French Derby. He was something of a mystery horse, since presumably his connections thought highly of him or they would not have let him run in such top-class events. The field was completed by Scherzo who before dead-heating with Bagdad for fourth place in the Grand Prix de Saint-Cloud had run unplaced in the Prix Ganay behind Carmarthen and Grandier. With the exception of Felicio II it appeared to be a very moderate field for such a famous race. Many good horses in recent years have won the Foy including Busted and Lorenzaccio, later to be the conqueror of Nijinsky in the 1970 Champion Stakes.

It is more than possible that Park Top's presence in the field frightened away other contenders. In spite of, or in some ways because of the fact that on all known form the mare should win, I was as nervous as ever. By now I had learnt that there were two different kinds of apprehension before Park Top took part in a race. On the major occasions such as the Coronation Cup, the Eclipse, and the King George VI and Queen Elizabeth Stakes, I was daunted by the very size of her task and of what she would have achieved were she to win. Victory in these great races meant so much that one could not believe it could actually happen. Whereas in the smaller races, such as the Prix de la Seine and now the Foy, I was anxious for fear of her failure and the knowledge that should she fail in the lesser task then the great objective, on this occasion the Arc, would be beyond reach. All the hopes accumulated over the weeks and months before would collapse in a matter of moments.

The fears grew that the hard-luck stories of Felicio's running at Ascot might be true, or that one or more of the others in the field would show a brilliance so far undisclosed, or worse still that our star had reached her zenith on July 26th and, as in the Vermeille two years previously, would now run far below her best.

Her appearance denied that any such doubts were justified. She still had the gleaming coat of high summer when Bernard and I visited her early in the morning of the race. She must have come to regard the Longchamp stables as a second home. This was her fourth visit there and she was bidding for her third successive victory on the Bois de Boulogne track.

All my anxieties were ill founded. Lester settled her down at the rear of the small field upsides with Felicio. Both were still at the back at the beginning of the straight. Finally Felicio made his effort at just the same moment as Lester made his. There followed a short sharp struggle. Then Park Top asserted her superiority and went on to win with a lot in hand by two lengths, with Felicio second and Pandora Bay third.

It was a convincing performance. The mare had shown she was as good as ever. The style of her victory won her many friends and the following morning *The Sporting Life* carried the bold headline "Park Top runs great Arc Trial".

Although, judged by the opposition she beat or the amount of stake money she won, the Prix Foy was not one of the mare's greatest victories, it gave me a disproportionate amount of pleasure. By her victory, and particularly by the style in which it was achieved, I knew she had a great chance of setting the seal on her career by capturing the Arc de Triomphe, which had not been won by a mare since La Sorelliana in 1953. I returned to London that evening in a state of euphoria. Park Top, now a worthy challenger for the Arc, had come a long way from the Mar Lodge Plate run that May evening at Windsor in 1967.

There were exactly four weeks before she was due to reappear at Longchamp. For the first two of these, I floated in pride and happiness. Total strangers would stop me in Bond Street and Piccadilly and ask how she was. She had become a national celebrity. Then as the day got nearer the well-known apprehension began to take over. In addition, Bernard and I had no definite assurance as to whether Lester would be able to take the ride. Earlier in the year, and before Park Top's King George VI and Queen Elizabeth Stakes victory he had undertaken to ride the Italian colt Bonconte di Montefeltro. This Charlottesville colt was the outstanding Italian three-year-old. He had won the Premio Pavioli, equivalent to our Two Thousand Guineas, and then the Italian Derby. Lester should have ridden him on both occasions but was unable to take the ride in the former as he was under suspension. He was, however, in the saddle for the Italian Derby. Two weeks later, again without Lester's services, Bonconte di Montefeltro won the valuable and prestigious Gran Premio di Italia run at Milan over 2,400 metres. After this, the colt's owner engaged Piggott to ride the horse in the Prix Royal-Oak, the French St. Leger, and then in the Arc de Triomphe. The horse ran disappointingly in the Royal-Oak finishing fourth behind Le Chouan, beaten more than three lengths. This race was run on September 14th, three weeks before the Arc, and after it Lester wished to be released from his obligation to ride the Italian colt in the Arc and to take the mount on Park Top.

Not unnaturally, Bonconte di Montefeltro's owner wished to hold Piggott to his agreement. Uncertainty then arose as to whether the contract was legally binding. In the end, after the Italian racing authorities had been consulted, Lester was allowed to take the ride on our mare. However, we were not sure that this would be the outcome until a few days before the race. As a precaution, Sandy Barclay was asked if he would ride for us should Piggott be unable to take the mount. He agreed and in fact rode her in one of her final gallops.

The Arc de Triomphe takes place on the Sunday following the Newmarket Cambridgeshire meeting. I had arranged to stay with Bernard for this and we were to fly over to Paris on the

Friday evening. Park Top, accompanied by Maureen and Michael Ryan, was to fly over early the same morning. Accompanying them would be the Newmarket Chief Inspector of police to provide security for the mare. Bernard felt that, with so much at stake, it would be foolish to leave anything to chance. He had asked the Inspector, an old friend, if he could recommend a suitable man from his force to keep an eye on the mare during the three nights she would be in France. Somewhat to his surprise the Inspector, a keen race-goer, said he would like the job himself.

Lester came to dinner at Northmore on the Wednesday and afterwards conversation turned to the great race. The chances of the various fancied horses were discussed and then Lester, from across the dining room table, said to me: "I think the mare will win – we will certainly be in the first three." I heard these words with mixed feelings. It was heartening to know he rated the mare's chances so highly, but such confidence seemed to be tempting the fates unnecessarily.

On the Friday morning I went over to Cambridge Airport to see the mare loaded into the aircraft and set off on her momentous journey. She was as cool and calm as ever, walking up the ramp into the aircraft without any fuss, just as if she was going into her box at Stanley House. Frank More O'Ferrall, an old friend and one of the mare's most devoted supporters, was with me and as the aeroplane took off, he put his hand on my shoulder saying: "Andrew, the next three days will possibly be the greatest in your life. No matter whether she wins or not, she has a great chance of achieving a lifetime's ambition for you. Savour every moment between now and 'the off'. Almost certainly, never again will you have a comparable experience."

I did my best to follow Frank's advice and it is certainly true that the emotion of the next 48 hours was something I have never experienced before or since. Bernard and I stayed as usual at the George V while Debo went to stay with her sister Diana outside Paris. The city was full of turf enthusiasts from all over the world, gathered for Europe's greatest race. The evenings were very social and I felt very proud to be introduced to visitors from America and elsewhere as the owner of the great Park Top.

With his usual forethought, Bernard had arranged for Park Top to be stabled in the yard of a small trainer at Maisons Laffitte. He was anxious to keep our champion away from the noise and excitement at Longchamp, particularly as there was to be racing on the Saturday when the race-course stables would be a hive of activity.

Early on the Saturday morning we drove down to see the mare. We found her and her attendants including the Chief Inspector happily ensconced in what was more of a farmyard than a racing stable. Park Top's box was big and airy and she had the most restful of companions, some cows, chickens and ducks. The Inspector, although not in uniform, appeared an incongruous figure among these rustic surroundings. The mare had travelled well and Maureen and Michael were well pleased with her. The only minor worry was that she had not quite finished her evening feed the night before.

We paid a second and final visit about 6.30 that evening. All was still well and this time Park Top had not left an oat. Among the chickens and ducks it was hard to imagine that we were in the presence of a great celebrity, one whose exploits and beautiful appearance had captured the imagination of the racing world. In the peace and quiet of those Maisons Laffitte stables, with only the quacking of the ducks to break the silence, it was difficult to take in that in a few hours Park Top would be lining up for the supreme test of her career.

Bernard and I lingered a long time in the stable yard, loath to leave its tranquillity and return to Paris and the agonising hours before the race.

Between our visits to Maisons Laffitte we went over yet again the formidable opposition the mare had to overcome if she was to win. There were 24 runners, consisting of 11 four-year-olds and upwards and 13 three-year-olds. So at last Park Top was to be pitted against the younger horses. There were twenty colts and four mares or fillies coming from France, England, Japan, Russia, Ireland and Italy. Of the French-trained contingent of 14 there was one seven-year-old, Fiasco, whose only noteworthy performance in recent years had been when running second, beaten by four lengths by Busted, in the Prix Foy two years previously. There were no French six-year-olds but two five-year-olds, Carmarthen and Grandier who between them had won many of the most famous middle-distance races in France. In their time they had both won the Prix Ganay and the Prix d'Harcourt, while Carmarthen had also won the Prix Daru, the Prix Prince d'Orange and the Prix Expres. The previous year he had finished third in the Arc to Vaguely Noble and Sir Ivor after which he had been fourth in the Washington International.

Grandier's other victories including the Prix Dollar and the Prix d'Ispahan together worth more than £30,000. In the 1968 French Free Handicap, for three-year-olds and upwards, Carmarthen had been allotted ten stone seven pounds which, taking weight-for-age into account, made him thirteen pounds below Vaguely Noble and nine pounds below Sir Ivor. Grandier had been allotted ten stone one.

Of the two French-trained four-year-olds, Candy Cane had spent most of his racing life in Ireland where he had been trained by J. M. Rogers for Lady Sassoon. As a two-year-old he had finished second to Sir Ivor in the seven-furlong National

Stakes. As a three-year-old he won the mile and a quarter Bally-moss Stakes, also at the Curragh, after which he was unplaced in the Irish 2,000 Guineas for which he started 6-4 on favourite. In the previous autumn he had finished third to Sir Ivor and Locris in the Champion Stakes, and won the £2,000 Royal Whip Stakes, at the Curragh over a mile and a half. After this, he was sent to France. The four-year-old mare Roselière, belonging to the late Charlie Engelhard and trained in France by George Bridgeland, had been the best of her sex in that country as a three-year-old, winning the Prix Vermeille and the French Oaks. In addition to that, she had finished fourth to Vaguely Noble in the Arc de Triomphe. She was the heaviest-weighted filly in the French Free Handicap, being given nine stone twelve. Taking into account weight-for-age, this put her above all the four-year-olds in the Handicap, and with sex allowance made her eight pounds below Vaguely Noble and four below Sir Ivor. As a four-year-old, after running twice unplaced, she had won the Prix De Pomone over one mile five furlongs at Deauville in August, so it looked as if she was returning to her brilliant best.

The seven French three-year-old colts were headed by Prince Regent and Goodley, the winners of the Irish Sweeps and French Derby respectively. As a two-year-old Prince Regent made a promising first appearance running third in the Prix Morny at Deauville, after which he had disappointed in finishing fifth of six in the six-furlong Prix de la Salamandre at Longchamp. This son of Right Royal opened his three-year-old career by winning the £50,000 Prix Lupin at Longchamp over a mile and two and a half furlongs. The going was heavy and he got the better of Caliban and Belbury by a head and a neck. He was then sent to Epsom, starting third favourite in the Derby at 13-2 and finishing third. Many considered the colt a very unlucky loser. He had a lot to do from Tattenham Corner and his task was made no easier by being bumped into twice while making his run. Prince Regent's next race was the Irish Sweeps Derby, where he turned the English Derby form upside down by beating the favourite Ribofilio by a length, with Reindeer five lengths behind third and Blakeney, the Derby winner, a further short head away fourth. Prince Regent had not run since his Curragh triumph.

The French Derby winner Goodley had started his three-year-old career by being second to Prince Regent in the Prix Goncourt and went on to beat Belbury in the Prix Mirage. This was followed by his victory in the Prix du Jockey-Club, the French Derby, where he got home by a short head and half a length from Beaugency and Djakao. There followed his narrow defeat by Felicio II in the Grand Prix de Saint-Cloud. The horse was then rested until the autumn when on his reappearance he got the better of a desperate finish with Carmarthen in the Prix du Prince d'Orange. The winners of the Irish and French Derbys were not the only French three-year-old colts with good chances of taking the Arc. There was the Val de Loir colt Chaparral, who had won the Grand Prix de Paris run over nearly two miles and worth £74,000. Although not officially a classic race, it is confined to three-year-old colts and fillies and can really be considered one. More recently, Chaparral had finished third, beaten a short head and a head in the Prix Royal-Oak, the winner being Le Chouan with Bonconte di Montefeltro fourth. Then there was Djakao, winner of the Grand Prix De Deauville in August following his third in the French Derby. Other dangers were Beaugency, winner of the Prix Hocquart and second to Goodley in the French Derby, and Belbury, winner of the Prix de Chantilly. The remaining French three-year-old colt Yelapa, had won the Grand Criterium at Longchamp the previous year and as a result had been given top weight in the Handicap Optional. The early part of his three-year-old career had been disappointing, but a week prior to the Arc he had shown signs of returning to his two-year-old form by finishing second to the English Derby runner-up Shoemaker, in the mile and three furlongs Prix Henri Delamarre.

The two French-trained three-year-old fillies Crepellana and Saraca were the best of their sex. Crepellana beat the latter by three quarters of a length in the French Oaks while Saraca reversed the placings by beating Crepallana by a short head in the Prix Vermeille.

Of the English contingent the senior in age was the six-year-old grey horse Copsale. The Arc de Triomphe would be the 38th race of his long and honourable career, during which time he had won eight races over distances from seven furlongs to a mile and five furlongs. In his early days he was trained by Ron Smyth at Epsom. His best achievement was winning the 1967 Magnet Cup at York. The following year, trained by Sam Armstrong at Newmarket, he had to wait until December for his first win of the year when, ridden by Piggott, he was a comfortable winner of the mile and a half Prix Bridaine at Saint-Cloud. However, it was as a six-year-old and running in France that this son of King's Bench really came into his own. After running second twice and third once carrying welterweights in decent handicaps in England, Sam sent him back to Saint-Cloud where he won his first of three successive races in France. This was the £5,000 Prix de Menil-Vicomte, run over rather more than nine and a half furlongs. Then followed his most important win to date when he took the Prix Maurice de Neuilly, also at Saint-Cloud. The race was worth £13,000 and it was over the same distance as his previous race. The third race of Copsale's hat-trick was the one mile five furlong Prix de Reux at Deauville, worth £4,500. Among those behind him that day were Soyeux. In his final outing before the Arc he had finished second in a mile and a half event at Maisons Laffitte, beaten a neck by the three-year-old A Chara. Beaugency was fifth, more than five lengths away. As can be seen, Copsale was a tough, much improved horse, but perhaps just lacking in class for a potential winner of the Arc.

Park Top was the only English five-year-old with her old rival Remand the only four-year-old. Jakie Astor had chosen the Cumberland Lodge for his horse's running-up race and he won it in spectacular style, beating Crozier by four lengths. The going had been firm but even so Remand's time of 2 minutes 31.83 seconds had been exceptionally fast, half a second faster than Park Top's time in the King George VI and Queen Elizabeth Stakes. The English three-year-olds were headed by the Derby winner Blakeney, who in his only outing since the Irish Sweeps Derby had run fifth in the St. Leger behind Intermezzo, Ribofilio and Prince Consort. Intermezzo was not in the Arc field but Ribofilio was. He had had an eventful season, which included the unenviable record of having started favourite in four Classics – the Two Thousand Guineas, the Derby, the St. Leger and the Irish Sweeps Derby – and winning none of them. His only two victories were in his first race of the season, the Ascot Two Thousand Guineas Trial in which he started at 5-1 on and beat two moderate rivals, and the mile and three quarter March Stakes at Goodwood at the end of August. On this occasion he started at 7-1 on to beat his only opponent. The horse had disgraced himself by refusing to gallop in the Two Thousand Guineas. He had, however, done well in the Derby, finishing fifth, about three and a half lengths behind Blakeney. Prince Regent had beaten him fair and square by a length in the Irish Sweeps Derby, while the colt again had to be content with second place in the St. Leger. This was an unsatisfactory race with a number of runners suffering interference in the straight as the early leaders fell back. Piggott had a very bad ride on the Engelhard horse and was considered to have been an unlucky loser. In spite of all the trials and tribulations that the colt had suffered during the season there seemed a distinct chance that Ribofilio might come good at last in the greatest race of the year. Bernard and I took comfort from the fact that Lester had chosen to ride Park Top when he could have had the mount on Ribofilio for the asking.

The remaining English colt Shoemaker, after running second to Blakeney in the Derby had again been second in the mile and a half Gordon Stakes at the Goodwood summer meeting. He was defeated by a good horse in Harmony Hall, who had won the Prince of Wales Stakes, also a mile and a half, at the Newmarket July meeting. Shoemaker ran a disappointing eighth in the St. Leger, but a week before the Arc had won the £11,500 Prix Henry Delamarre.

Of the other runners Speed Symboli had had one race since the King George VI and Queen Elizabeth Stakes, running unplaced in the Grand Prix de Deauville. I have already given in some detail the exploits of the Italian Bonconte di Montefeltro. There remained two four-year-olds, the Russian Zbor and the Irish Levmoss. Zbor was by the Grand Prix de Paris and Ascot Gold Cup winner Balto and had won two of the chief middle distance races in the USSR earlier in the year. The previous season he had won the Russian St. Leger. This was his first venture in Western Europe and he was a completely unknown quantity. The same could not be said of Levmoss who we last heard of the previous August when he had beaten Canterbury and Park Top in the Oxfordshire Stakes at Newbury. After this he had returned to Ireland and on his next appearance at the Curragh had run down the field in the mile and a half Blandford Stakes. He then went back to France for the French St. Leger in which he finished third.

His final run as a three-year-old was back in Ireland when winning the two mile Leopardstown November Handicap, from a field of thirty-one, by four lengths, under the enormous weight for a three-year-old of nine stones four pounds. This was a tremendous performance and boded well for his future as a Cup horse. He reappeared on March 29th in the seven furlong Gladness Stakes at the Curragh, where he was ignored in the Market and made no show. A month later he ran third in the Prix Jean Prat, a race of just under two miles, at Longchamp, behind another four-year-old, the Aga Khan's Zamazaan and a five-year-old, Samos III. After this Levmoss was unbeaten for the rest of the season. He returned to France for the two and a half mile Prix Cadran, the French equivalent of the Ascot Gold Cup, where he reversed the placings in the Jean Prat by beating Zamazaan and Samos by a head and neck. Next came the Ascot Gold Cup when, starting at the fifteen to eight favourite, he beat Torpid, who had been fourth in the Cadran, by four lengths. His last run before the Arc was when he won the Leinster Handicap, of a mile and three quarters worth only £798, at the Curragh. He was carrying ten stones ten pounds, and won by three lengths but in spite of his Cadran and Gold Cup victories, and presumably because of the enormous weight he was set to carry, Levmoss did not start favourite, being returned at nine to two.

This then was the line up our champion had to face on the afternoon of October 5th. I have probably given the performances of her opponents in too great detail but I am anxious to show that if, with the exception of Felicio II, she was competing against second class opposition in the King George VI and Queen Elizabeth Stakes, the field of the Arc was of superb quality. In particular the best three-year-olds in Europe were turning out, including the winners of the English, Irish, French and Italian Derbys, supported by the winner of the Grand Prix de Paris and the unlucky second in the English St. Leger, as well as the two outstanding French three-year-old fillies.

To Bernard's and my regret Wolver Hollow had been retired to stud immediately after his victory in the Eclipse. Park Top was thus denied a chance of proving how unlucky she had been that day at Sandown. As Wolver Hollow was by Sovereign Path it is unlikely he would have stayed the mile and a half but we would both have dearly liked to see him in the field. In such ante-post betting as there had been Prince Regent was made favourite with, until his defeat in the Prix Royal-Oak, Bonconte di Montefeltro second choice and Park Top third. I had had the biggest bet of my life at 6-1, placing it directly after the Prix Foy.

With the mare at Maisons Laffitte rather than Longchamp, Bernard and I did not pay her our usual early morning day-of-the-race visit. I slept as late as I could, then we all lunched with my former brother-in-law Derek Jackson and set off early for the Bois de Boulogne as Bernard had Shaft running in the second race. The longest afternoon of my life had begun.

Lester won the first race, the famous five-furlong Prix de L'Abbaye by three quarters of a length on Tower Walk trained by Geoffrey Barling at Newmarket. He then won the second on Shaft by half a length. Delighted as Debo and I were that Bernard should win such a good race, it seemed as if Piggott might be having too much good fortune too early in the afternoon. The possibility of the mare's success thus continued to recede in my mind as it had done ever since I arrived in Paris two days earlier. Then Piggott won the third race, a valuable mile event for fillies, on the French trained Vela. After that I knew in my bones and in my heart that Park Top would not win.

I had not seen the earlier races as I was watching the mare being led round outside the race-course stables. Bernard gave me the news and I think he too felt our quest was now in vain. By this time I was numb and the only emotion I showed was irritation of which Debo got the lion's share. In France the horses do not appear in the public parade ring until just before the jockeys are due to mount so we seemed to spend hours as the mare and her rivals walked round and round the stables. Finally it was time for Bernard to saddle her and then she was led out into the public gaze.

Lester appeared almost at once. I muttered through my teeth some unwilling congratulations on his great achievement of riding a hat-trick at Longchamp on an Arc de Triomphe day. Then he was in the saddle and on his way to the parade in front of the stands.

Although the French racing authorities had supplied me with every sort of badge for the stand reserved for owners of horses running in the Arc, I had failed to find out where it was. The crowds were enormous and the stands completely packed. For a few moments it looked as if we were not going to get a proper view of the race, then Debo remembered that Derek Jackson had said we might go to his box. This took a little time to find but eventually we all squeezed into it, although as a result I fear Derek and his wife did not see much of the contest.

The difficulty of finding somewhere to watch from meant there was something to occupy my mind during those last few agonising minutes before the off. By the time we had got to Derek's box the parade was over and the horses already at the start. The loading into the stalls took a surprisingly short time. Park Top was drawn on the inside of the field. A great roar announced the off and the moment had arrived that had been occupying my mind to an ever-greater extent since the day in early June when Park Top had electrified us all by the brilliance of her win in the Coronation Cup.

Bonconte di Montefeltro set off in front at a tremendous gallop with Blakeney, Chaparral and Levmoss well up from the start. As the field went past the stands on the far side of the course, heading in the opposite direction, I could see Park Top on the rails well to the back of the field. She was still there when the horses reappeared into view after going behind the copse at the top of the hill at the far end of the course, with Prince Regent just in front of her. The order remained unchanged as the field swung right-handed round the long downhill turn into the straight. As they were rounding the bend, I just caught a glimpse of Piggott still on the rails and still a long way back. A sense of despair came over me. Not only were we not going to win but so far as the mare was concerned, the race was going to be a ghastly anti-climax.

The field levelled out in the straight. The Italian colt was still out in front, with Chaparral, Shoemaker and Levmoss, the latter on the rails close behind. Where, oh God, where was Park Top? Then I saw her behind a wall of horses in the middle of the course, with Lester looking desperately for an opening. By this time Levmoss had shot clear of the field, pursued by Grandier and Chaparral. I had lost sight of Lester again, and now the race was in its closing stages with Williamson riding Levmoss for the line like a man inspired.

It was all over, the mare would finish in the ruck. The dream turned to nightmare, the whole house of cards was collapsing in front of our eyes. Sickening waves of disappointment began to flow over me. Then it happened.

With a furlong to go Lester, by bringing Park Top to the wide outside, had at last got a clear run. For once the phrase "to set a horse alight" was literally true. At Lester's urging Park Top appeared to be flying. Her straw colours looked like a meteor flashing over the green Longchamp turf. The winning post was too close for her to catch Levmoss. She could not win but we started to cheer in a frenzy of excitement. Rarely can a horse have shown such speed and courage as she did in covering the last 200 yards of the course. At the post Levmoss had a rapidly diminishing three-quarters of a length to spare. Three lengths away, third, came Grandier, Grandier who a furlong out had been lengths in front of Park Top. Now he was lengths behind.

*　　　*　　　*

The finish of the 1969 Prix de L'Arc de Triomphe will be talked of as long as men go racing. Certainly, there was to be endless discussion about it in the days that followed. At the moment that Levmoss and Park Top went past the post, I was completely happy. Who cared whether she had won or not? Park Top with her burst of speed had made the finest field of thoroughbreds in Europe look like hacks.

We hurried down the stands to meet her. Lester must have pulled her up very quickly for he was the first to return to the unsaddling enclosure. I do not remember him saying anything, though he may well have done. I do not think any of us were at that moment disappointed. The exhilaration of the mare's fantastic finish was still with us. Certainly, I was too proud of her to feel any anguish at her narrow defeat.

I flew back to London in the evening. Peter O'Sullevan was on the aeroplane. He commiserated with me on our defeat and said how unlucky he thought the mare had been. He also told me that he had seen Lester in the weighing room immediately after the race who had told him that he blamed himself for the mare's defeat. This was generous of Lester, but the information and Peter's obvious dismay at the manner of the mare's defeat caused me, for the first time, to realise fully how near to success, a success we had all so dearly longed for, the mare had come. Earlier, before leaving the race-course, I had run into a friend from Ireland. She too had commiserated with me on Park Top's unlucky run. I had dismissed her kind condolences and assured her that I was thrilled and delighted by my horse's performance, at which the lady got a bit vexed and said : "Oh, for God's sake, don't be so damn sporting about it." The truth was I was not being a good loser. I was still dazzled by the mare's unforgettable finish. Now, on my way back to London, I did begin to feel regret that Park Top had in all probability been denied the triumph she deserved. Later my thoughts turned to Bernard, Maureen, Michael and everyone at Stanley House stables. To Bernard the defeat must have been cruel beyond understanding. Through the months of his illness, he had given his whole being to the care of Park Top. From early spring until well into the autumn, she had been his paramount concern – now he had been robbed of the crown of success in the race that mattered above all others. At the time and afterwards he never complained over how fortune had cheated him of the achievement of a lifetime.

Not everyone regarded Park Top as an unlucky loser. It was pointed out that Levmoss had passed the post full of running and since he was an out-and-out stayer Williamson could have got something more out of him to resist the mare's challenge. Having seen the film of the race on countless occasions I do not accept this argument. From the moment Levmoss struck the front early in the straight, Williamson was driving him for all he was worth. He was making full use of the colt's unlimited stamina and throughout the last two furlongs the colt was galloping as fast as he could. It is common enough to see a horse who is staying on appearing to fly when catching another who is tiring towards the end of a race. The whole point of the finish of the 1969 Arc is that Levmoss was not tiring, he was full of running and yet, in the closing stages, he appeared to be marking time as the mare relentlessly closed with him. She was gaining yards with every stride. As to the difficult question of Lester's tactics, I do not blame him for the mare's defeat. She had always to be ridden from behind, and as Lester has said of her she knew as much about racing as he did. He was therefore entirely justified in letting her run her own race. He knew of the staggering speed she had at her command when the moment came, even in races like the Arc which are run at a tremendous pace from start to finish. Levmoss's time broke the then record for the course. In such circumstances there will always be horses among the leaders in the early stages of the race falling back beaten when the final straight is reached. As often as not, as we have seen in the running of the Eclipse and the King George VI and Queen Elizabeth Stakes, an opening is more likely to occur on the rails than in the middle of the field. It is true that Lester could have put the mare on the outside from the start but by doing so he would have lost many lengths on the long right-handed bend to the straight. Later in this story, when it comes to the 1970 Coronation Cup, I shall be critical of Lester's riding, but in the Arc I have no fault to find with him. A few days after the race, a friend in condoling with me added : "Well, anyway, Andrew, you are pretty intolerable as it is – you would have been quite intolerable if you had won." I accept that for myself, but it was of no consolation to Bernard, Maureen and all the others who were concerned with the care of the mare for the four years in which she resided at Stanley House stables.

Finally in assessing the result of the Arc it is worthwhile looking back to the previous occasion when Levmoss and Park Top had met. This was the Oxfordshire Stakes at Newbury rather more than a year previously. I have already dealt at length with that race and readers may recollect that Park Top was third to her Arc conqueror, beaten a neck and a head at five pounds worse terms than weight-for-age. The race was run on soft going over one mile five furlongs and sixty yards. Conditions were thus all in favour of the colt, while the mare's best distance was a mile and a half and she liked fast ground. In the Arc it was the other way round. The mare had everything right for her while the one and a half miles on the best of going must have been on the short side for a Cadran and Ascot Gold Cup winner. Furthermore she was meeting the Irish hope on five pounds better terms. Strictly on the Oxfordshire Stakes running the mare should have reversed the placings with Levmoss but provided both gave of their best it is clear that there would not have been a great deal in it.

If Park Top had won she would have been retired at once, and this would have been the end of her story. As it was, she was to run in five more races which provide, if not on quite the same scale, enough drama for a book of their own.

Park Top had been entered for the Champion Stakes over a mile and a quarter to be run at Newmarket on October 18th. A week or so after the Arc Bernard telephoned to say she was amazingly well and had shown no ill effects from her hard race in Paris. He suggested she should take her chance in the Champion. I was delighted with the idea. I had made up my mind to retire her at the end of the season, and was anxious that her last race should be a winning one. What better than to capture the Champion, a famous and very valuable event. So it was settled, with the proviso that she would only run if Bernard was absolutely happy that she was in a condition to do herself full justice.

The opposition was strong but on known form there did not appear to be any obvious danger provided the mare gave her true running. Her chief opponent appeared to be Connaught who many regarded as better over a mile and a quarter than a mile and a half. In evidence of this was his highly impressive five-lengths victory over Wolver Hollow at Royal Ascot in the Prince of Wales Stakes over that distance. Since then Jim Joel's St. Paddy colt had failed to win but had run two good races, especially when third to Karabas and Hotfoot in the mile and a quarter Scarborough Stakes at Doncaster. Karabas was the other star in Bernard's stable, who was to go on to win the Washington International at Laurel Park. In Connaught's other race, his last before the Champion, he had run very well to finish second to Jimmy Reppin in the mile Queen Elizabeth II Stakes at Ascot. It was a good performance since Jimmy Reppin, in addition to being third to Sir Ivor and Petingo in the previous year's Two Thousand Guineas, had proved himself to be one of the best milers in the country, and a mile was probably too short to see Connaught at his best. Hogarth was again to be in the line-up, having his first run in England since his third in the King George VI and Queen Elizabeth Stakes. From France came the five-year-old Locris, who in his last race had finished fifth behind Habitat in the race that had given Lester his fourth winning ride on Arc de Triomphe day. Previous to that, Locris had been second to Grandier in the one mile one furlong Prix D'Ispahan and before that second in the Prix Dollar. He was among the best of the middle-distance horses in France. In the 1968 French Free Handicap he had been given ten stone three pounds, while in the 1969 Free Handicap he was to be placed five pounds below Park Top.

Of the two other four-year-olds, Lorenzaccio, by Klairon out of a The Phoenix mare, was a pretty useful performer trained by Noel Murless for Charles St. George. As a three-year-old he had won the mile and one furlong Prix Jean Prat worth £13,000. He had not won during the present season but had put up some good performances in high class company, including running second in the Royal Hunt Cup at Ascot under nine stone, and fourth to Habitat, Jimmy Reppin and Tower Walk in the £7,500 Lockinge Stakes at Newbury in May when he had Wolver Hollow ten lengths behind him. In 1970, as a five-year-old, he was to achieve lasting fame by defeating the great Nijinsky in that year's Champion.

The remaining four-year-old Principal Boy had earned his

place in the field by beating the English and Irish 2,000 Guineas and Royal Ascot St. James Palace Stakes winner Right Tack in the mile and a quarter Peter Hastings Stakes a month before at Newbury.

The field was completed by two French-trained three-year-old fillies, Hecuba and Flossy. In her last race Hecuba had won the Prix De La Nonette worth more than £6,000 and run over rather more than a mile and a quarter at Longchamp. Earlier in the year she had been well beaten by both Crepellana and Saraca. Of Flossy, other than that she was by a horse called Spywell out of a Pot Luck mare, little was known. Certainly she did not appear a serious threat in the parade before the race, being small and of no great quality.

October 18th, 1969, was one of those days that happens to all of us. It was unmitigated disaster from start to finish. The running of the Champion coincided with the annual one-day Equestrian Event held at Chatsworth. Her Royal Highness Princess Anne was among the competitors and Her Majesty the Queen was staying for the occasion. She had graciously permitted me to absent myself from the proceedings to see Park Top run, only asking me to watch carefully the running of her horse St. Patrick's Blue, who was a fancied candidate for the Cesarewitch to be run prior to the Champion. Accordingly I set off in my customary subdued and apprehensive state. Our decision to run the mare so soon after the Arc caused some criticism and I was anxious that this should prove unjustified. Far more important, I was desperately keen for the mare to be compensated for her ill-fortune at Longchamp by winning this famous race before she was retired.

All went well until about 20 miles from Newmarket when my car suddenly emitted a loud bang and a thin cloud of blue smoke rose up from the bonnet. The car did not actually stop and Joe gently pulled up. He took a look at the engine but could not discover the cause of the trouble. As it could still just go we continued, but at a maximum speed of 15 miles an hour for the remainder of the journey. Fortunately, I had plenty of time but the last twenty miles took over an hour, during which the Cesarewitch was won and lost. For the last few miles it began to look as if I would not get to the course in time to see Park Top run, however, I arrived just as the horses were leaving the paddock. I found Bernard and, as at Longchamp, we watched the race together, a custom we had abandoned as unlucky earlier in the mare's career.

Park Top was drawn number seven in the field of ten, which meant she was towards the outside, between Shoemaker and Connaught. Flossy had the berth nearest the stand rails. Connaught set off in front pressed by Hogarth, Shoemaker and Principal Boy. Approaching the bushes, with two furlongs to run, Piggott made his move on the outside and a great cheer went up as the mare closed the gap with the leaders in her usual effortless style. For a moment it looked as if all was well, and she would come home unchallenged. Then, coming down the hill, with more than a furlong to run, Deforge loosed Flossy on the inside. As the filly fairly flew down the hill, Park Top struggled gallantly for some strides to match the devastating speed of her French rival, but she had to give the younger horse best and Flossy went on to win comfortably by two lengths with Lorenzaccio four lengths behind Park Top in third place. She had started at 85-40 on, with six to one bar her. Flossy was not unbacked at 100-7.

It was a bitter blow. For the first time in her eight races that season, Park Top had been beaten fair and square without there being any question of luck playing any part in the result.

There was no time for any post-mortems for after the Queen's kindness in allowing me to see the race, the least I could do was to be back at Chatsworth in time for dinner. Joe had left the car in a garage and he and I returned in a ramshackle taxi. There were patches of autumn fog all the way home and to my general misery at Park Top's defeat was added the anxiety that I would be late. However, about the only thing in the day that did go right was that I got back just in time. Part of the evening was spent in watching films of the mare's earlier triumphs, and seeing again her glorious victories in the Coronation Cup and the King George VI and Queen Elizabeth Stakes eased the pain of the day's defeat.

During the days that followed the Champion, I had a chance to analyse the form. I came to the conclusion to which I still hold, that probably Park Top ran up to her best form, allowing for the fact that, by now, a mile and a quarter was too short a trip for her. My reasoning was based on the positions at the finish of the other runners whom the mare had beaten when they had met before, Hogarth, Connaught and Shoemaker.

She had defeated all of these in the Champion more easily than when they had last met. Hogarth, who had finished fourth, was seven lengths behind the mare as compared with the two lengths beating he had received in the King George VI and Queen Elizabeth Stakes and the three lengths in the Eclipse. Connaught was the best part of ten lengths away compared with the two and a quarter lengths in the Coronation Cup, while Shoemaker was beaten out of sight as he had been in the Arc.

It seemed clear that we had been beaten by a better horse on the day. After the Champion, Flossy returned to the obscurity from whence she came, and as far as I know has never been heard of since. The time of 2 minutes 7.06 seconds was fast, being nearly three seconds under the average. As I have said, Flossy did not run unbacked and it became known after the race that she had done a brilliant gallop with Candy Cane prior to that horse finishing fourth in the Arc. There is no doubt that on the day it mattered, M. Boutin produced Flossy in a condition in which she was able to beat Park Top at her own game with an exceptionally brilliant burst of speed in the closing stages of the race.

History was to show that the mighty Nijinsky was to suffer a similar fate the following year. He, too, had been narrowly and, some say, unluckily beaten in the Arc. Then, with the Champion apparently at his mercy, he had gone under to Lorenzaccio. In 1973 the peerless Allez France suffered the same indignity, defeat in the Arc, followed by another in the Champion.

1970

Ending Up

The mare's five-year-old career ended in disappointment, just as in the two previous seasons : nevertheless from eight starts she had won five times and finished second in the other three. Of those defeats, that in the Eclipse had been a desperately unlucky one, In another, the Arc de Triomphe, many good judges considered her equally unlucky. It was only in the last, the Champion, that she was well and truly beaten on merit. Furthermore, with the exception of her first outing, she had taken on the best horses, both colts and fillies, in Europe on equal terms. Her ability and courage received their just reward when she was made the Flat Race-horse of the Year. This was a striking tribute since Levmoss, by winning the Ascot Gold Cup in his only race in England also qualified for the award. In addition her rivals for the much-coveted trophy naturally included the winners of all five of the English classics, among whom was Sleeping Beauty, the late Lord Rosebery's lovely filly who had won both the 1,000 Guineas and the Oaks. I like to feel that the racing press, when voting for the mare, felt that her exploits throughout the season deserved some special recognition, even if judged strictly on performance the award should have gone to Levmoss. As a result, a half-size replica of the Horse of the Year challenge trophy, a bronze of a horse coming in after a race with the jockey touching his cap in acknowledgement of victory, sculpted by Jean Walwyn, stands surrounded by the Coronation, King George VI and Queen Elizabeth Stakes and the Long-champ cups on the sideboard at Chatsworth.

In retrospect I seem to have made up my mind to keep Park Top in training as a six-year-old surprisingly quickly. There were none of the agonising deliberations as to whether to send her to stud that had preceded the decision to keep her at Stanley House for the 1969 season. At the time, her defeats in the Arc and more especially her eclipse in the Champion by Flossy rankled, and I was determined that provided she remained sound and continued to love racing, she should wipe out those unhappy memories by gracing the race-courses of England and France for one more year. If there had been muted criticism of my keeping the mare in training as a five-year-old, there was now a positive torrent of disapproval when it became known she was to stay in training for yet another season. One doughty and distinguished Life Peeress attacked me violently about it in the lobby of the House of Lords, to the extent that I feared she was going to report me to the Royal Society for the Prevention of Cruelty to Animals or even the Lord Chancellor. This indigna-tion was yet another mark of the esteem and affection in which Park Top was held.

Many of her admirers felt that she had done more than enough and had fully earned an honourable retirement to the stud paddocks. These critics did not worry me, since I knew the mare would never be allowed to race unless Bernard was fully satisfied that she would run in the manner that had earned her fame and glory. If Bernard heard the criticisms he kept his own council and in any case he was never the man to be swayed by the opinions of others.

Winter came and went and by March Bernard and I were dis-cussing the season's campaign. As in the previous year the Coronation Cup was to be the first main objective. We were hoping to emulate Petite Etoile by winning the Epsom race two years in succession. Again as in 1969, the plan was to give her one tuning-up race, if possible a relatively easy one, before tackling the Epsom semi-classic.

Park Top had wintered well and came to hand early. The original idea was to run her in the mile and a half John Porter Stakes at Newbury on Saturday April 18th. This is a condition race for four-year-olds and upwards. From what could be gathered of the likely composition of the field it did not appear that the race would take a lot of winning. The Spring had been wet and at the Newmarket Craven meeting immediately before Newbury the going was soft. I was staying with Bernard and though he was anxious for the mare to run at Newbury the continuing rain made him increasingly doubtful as to whether it would be wise. She needed fast ground to be at her best and the soft going at Newbury in the Oxfordshire Stakes and at Ascot in the Cumberland Lodge in 1968 had certainly contributed to her defeats in those races. A decision was made more difficult as the announcement at the beginning of the month that the 1969 Flat Race-horse of the Year was to reappear at Newbury had caused great interest in the racing world. A big crowd could be expected to turn up to see her. Neither Bernard nor I wanted to disappoint the mare's innumerable fans by a last-minute change of plan, so we delayed making a decision as long as possible. Park Top was therefore sent to the Berkshire track.

On the Friday, the going was officially described as 'dead' but more rain fell during the afternoon and evening and by Saturday morning it had become heavy. Reluctantly we decided not to let her run. Charlie Toller, the Clerk of the Course, agreed that as the mare was on the course she should be allowed to be led round the preliminary parade ring for a time during the early part of the afternoon and an announcement to this effect was made over the loudspeakers. A large crowd quickly gathered to see Park Top, who as always showed that she was well aware of the admiration she evoked. I basked in her reflected glory without a care in the world. In fact, I spent a glorious afternoon feeling very different to what I would have had she been competing. My day was made when I overheard a tweeded lady pointing out the mare to a small boy and saying: "There is the greatest horse in Europe and you are very lucky to have seen her."

Having to miss the John Porter posed a problem since it was essential to give Park Top a race before she went to Epsom and there were not many suitable ones to choose from. After her unhappy experience in the Ormonde in 1968 neither Bernard nor I had much enthusiasm for her to return to Chester. The Coronation Stakes at Sandown was over a mile and a quarter, a distance we now thought too short for her. The mile and a half Jockey Club Stakes at the Newmarket Guineas meeting did, however, fit the bill, and since Sleeping Partner was to be in the field it was tempting to take her on. The race would also afford an opportunity of renewing rivalry with Blakeney.

There were also a number of races in France. In the end, Bernard chose La Coupe De Longchamp to be run on Thursday May 7th. As in the past, prize money was an important consideration in coming to this decision. The Jockey Club Stakes was worth £3,300 to the winner while La Coupe was worth more than £6,000. An added attraction of the latter race was that the mare had shown how much she liked the course in the Bois de Boulogne.

Finally, then as now, I regarded the Newmarket Rowley Mile Course as unlucky. So it was to be back to Paris.

We did not follow our usual routine of going over to France the evening before the race as I had people staying for Chester Races. In fact, I won a race there on the Wednesday.

I arranged to meet Bernard on the course and flew over from Manchester very early on the Thursday morning, uncertain whether to regard my win the previous day as a good omen or a case of using up good luck before it was really needed.

I spent the morning wandering round the Ile De Saint Louis and looking at Notre Dame where High Mass was being celebrated. But my mind was not fully occupied by the great Cathedral and the glorious singing of the choir. My thoughts kept coming back to the race in the afternoon. Although the opposition did not appear formidable, there was more than the race at stake. The result would show, as only a race can, whether I had been justified in keeping the mare in training as a six-year-old. She had pleased Bernard in her work at Newmarket but, as every race-goer knows, the race-course is the only true test and in this case would provide proof or otherwise as to whether the mare was still a great race-horse.

There were only three other runners, all colts and all trained in France. Chaparral had finished sixth in the Arc in the previous year. He had had one outing in the current season, finishing second, beaten two lengths, in a field of six in the Prix Jean Prat of just under two miles. Of the other two runners Le Chouan had won the French St. Leger the previous year and had finished third in the Jean Prat a long way behind Chaparral. Both these four-year-olds had the Prix du Cadran as their main objective – indeed they were to finish first and second in this French equivalent of the Ascot Gold Cup. While the one mile five furlongs of La Coupe was perhaps a shade further than Park Top's best distance it would suit her better than the colts who were out-and-out stayers and were in the field that afternoon primarily as part of their preparation for the Cadran. Unless Soyeux who made up the field had improved a great deal there was nothing to fear from his running in the 1969 King

George VI and Queen Elizabeth Stakes. On all the known form, therefore, Park Top had the race at her mercy.

My anxieties were the same as in those other races in which she had appeared to have an outstanding chance. Failure to win could only mean that she had deteriorated since the previous year. By the time the horses were being loaded into the stalls I was wishing with all my heart that Park Top was many miles away on the other side of the Channel grazing happily in the paddocks of the stud to which she had been sent to be covered.

Once more my fears were groundless. The mare put up a tremendous performance, showing all her old brilliance. Her devastating speed proved far too much for her three rivals in a race that was virtually a repeat performance of the Prix Foy in the previous September. Lester kept her in the rear until well into the straight and then giving her a little rein she swept contemptuously past the colts to win hard-held by half a length from Chaparral with Le Chouan three quarters of a length away third.

Each of Park Top's 13 victories had their own savour and delight. In La Coupe the mare's win gave me very special pleasure because once again she had not let me down, even though I had asked a great deal of her. Once again she had vindicated Bernard's infallible judgement by putting up a performance equal to her achievements of the year before. The critics were silenced and her admirers became more ardent than ever. The sporting press gave her unqualified praise while Lester in a letter to me written shortly afterwards wrote: "The old mare is as good as ever."

Thinking about the future on the journey home the mare's prospects appeared dazzling. Once again the racing world, at least as far as the older horses were concerned, appeared to be at her mercy. The Coronation Cup seemed a formality. Then there was the prospect of a meeting with the mighty Nijinsky, who had recently run away with the Two Thousand Guineas, in the King George VI and Queen Elizabeth Stakes at Ascot in July. It all seemed too good to be true : and it was.

It had become clear some time beforehand that we would have few opponents in the Coronation Cup. After the way Park Top had trounced them in the Arc few of the previous year's three-year-olds were anxious to renew their challenge, while none of the older horses appeared to have any chance of lowering her colours now that she had shown she was as good as ever. Up to the weekend prior to the Epsom meeting, it looked as if she would only have two opponents, the four-year-old Shoemaker and the five-year-old Swallow Tail II. The former, in addition to being second to Blakeney in the 1969 Derby, had won the Prix Henry Delamarre from Yelapa at Longchamp at the end of September 1969, before running unplaced in the Arc. In the current season, he had had two runs, finishing second to Hot Foot in the Coronation Stakes at Sandown, the race in which Karabas had started the odds-on favourite only to run one of his few bad races. Shoemaker then went to Saint-Cloud to win the Prix Jean de Chaudenay, again beating Yelapa. Swallow Tail II was a good handicapper who had won four races as a four-year-old and who had shown his well-being by taking the John Davies Stakes, a mile and a half handicap at Haydock, a fortnight earlier. However, he appeared to be outclassed by both the mare and Shoemaker.

In the week before Epsom fate took a hand in events in the form of a transport strike in France which affected racing there.

Noel Murless had intended to send his good four-year-old Caliban to France to run on the Sunday before the Coronation Cup. The strike forced him to change this plan and Caliban was sent to Epsom instead. This colt by Ragusa out of a Court Martial mare had been lightly raced, winning one of his only two races as a two-year-old while in four starts as a three-year-old he had won the Blue Riband Trial Stakes at the Epsom Spring meeting, after which he ran sixth to Right Tack in the 2,000 Guineas. There followed two excellent performances in France. In the first of these Caliban ran Prince Regent to a head in the Prix Lupin, recognised as a major trial for the French Derby. Caliban ran in the French Classic and although he was only sixth to Goodley he was beaten by less than three lengths. This was his last race as a three-year-old and the Coronation Cup was his first outing at four.

I have already described the build-up of differing emotions in the days prior to Park Top's appearance on a race-course. The time before her attempt to win the Coronation Cup for a second time followed the usual pattern. On this occasion the state of the going was an additional anxiety. The ground was firm when the Epsom meeting opened on the Wednesday and this was reflected by the fact that Nijinsky won the Derby in nearly four seconds faster time than Blakeney a year earlier. While Bernard was completely satisfied with the mare's well-being and she had given him no anxiety since the Longchamp race, he would have preferred a little more give in the ground but the state of the going did not worry him enough to consider not running her.

With only four runners the preliminaries took less time than usual and the field was on its way with a minimum of delay. With such a small field the pace was likely to be slow, just as it had been in the Hardwicke at Royal Ascot in 1969. Barclay on Caliban set off in front at no great gallop, followed by Swallow Tail, Park Top and Shoemaker. Caliban continued in front without noticeably increasing the pace all the way up the hill and then down to Tattenham Corner. Remembering how the mare had cut down Chicago in a few strides in the Hardwicke after a desperately slow run race, the dismal gallop set by Barclay did not worry me. The order remained the same as they turned into the straight with Caliban lobbing along at the head of affairs. As the field approached the two-furlong marker, Duncan Keith on Shoemaker made his effort, passing both Park Top and Swallow Tail. The latter immediately dropped out of contention.

The crucial moment came as Shoemaker went past the mare. For a moment it looked as if Lester was going to go in pursuit of Caliban at the same moment as Duncan Keith. He pulled out a little from the rails as if to challenge on the outside, but then appeared to change his mind and, resuming his 'man of marble' pose, switched her back to the rails for another hundred and fifty yards or so.

It is impossible to think coherently in the fleeting moments when races are won and lost, but when Lester appeared to abandon his idea of pursuing Shoemaker in challenging Caliban, I was filled with dismay, as he appeared to be denying the mare her chance of victory. Barclay had really got to work on the Murless horse more than a furlong out and was making the best of his way home, with Shoemaker in hot pursuit but making little impression.

Finally, with less than a furlong left Piggott started to ride the mare for all he was worth. She responded as gamely and as brilliantly as ever, making up ground in the same devastating way as in the Arc. In a few strides she was past Shoemaker but the post came just too soon. Gaining every split second, Park Top had reached Caliban's quarters as they went over the line. The official distance was three-quarters of a length.

In many ways, the finish was very similar to that of the Arc but although Park Top had less ground to make up on Caliban than she had on Levmoss, she had less distance to do it in. It was a bitter blow, for without doubt in another two or three strides she would have won. In my view, on this occasion Lester left his effort too late and did not give the mare a fair chance. He asked too much even of her brilliant speed and acceleration.

On his return Lester told us that the mare had not acted on the ground. It is true that Epsom was not the ideal course for her. She preferred flat, galloping courses. Still, she had acted well enough when putting paid to Mount Athos and Connaught the previous year. Equally it is true, as I have already said, that the going was firmer than we would have liked, but it had not prevented her from keeping in close touch with the leaders throughout the race, and with two furlongs to go she was in an ideal position from which to go on and win her race. Had Lester followed Duncan Keith when the latter made his challenge I remain convinced the mare would have won her second Coronation Cup as easily as her first. Lester came in for some fairly general criticism, although there were those who felt that Barclay, by dictating a slow pace until well into the straight, had stolen the race more than Lester had lost it. I do not think this argument is valid since it is disproved by the way the mare had won the Hardwicke, a race run in an almost identical fashion. It is true Caliban's winning time was 15 seconds slower than Nijinsky's in the Derby and 8 seconds slower than Lupe's in the Oaks, but equally the Hardwicke had been run in 22 seconds worse than the average for the course, although the going had been good.

As after her defeats in the Eclipse and the Arc, Park Top's glory was in no way diminished by the result. Equally I was in no position to complain about my luck, my good fortune in owning her far outweighing any misfortunes Park Top may have had when carrying my colours in some of her most important races. For the mare herself, this defeat coming on top of those in the Arc and the Eclipse, was nevertheless a cruel stroke of fortune. She was so courageous and so brilliant, and above all so willing to give her best time and time again that she deserved better of fate. To those lucky enough to see her on the race-course she was as great in defeat as in victory, but the record books print only the result and not the story behind it. I am only sad that long after my mare and her countless admirers are dead and gone, students of racing who observe that Park Top, unlike Petite Etoile, narrowly failed to win her second successive Coronation Cup will have no one to tell them that this defeat was not due to any failure on her part.

It is difficult to be impartial when one is deeply involved, and I am very ready to agree that I may have been unduly harsh on Lester in his riding of the mare that unhappy day at Epsom. The future was to show that both Bernard's anxiety about the firmness of the going, and Lester's assertion that she could not act on the ground, were borne out by what followed.

At the end of the week Bernard told me the mare's front legs were very sore and that she was thoroughly stumped up. The only cure was a long rest, so the remainder of her summer campaign had to be abandoned and the clash with Nijinsky in the King George VI and Queen Elizabeth Stakes never took place.

It was not until August that Bernard put Park Top back into strong work. She stood up to it well and by the beginning of September we were once more discussing her future. Bernard had left her in the Arc but I could see he was not keen to run her. No doubt he felt that after her Epsom setback he could not subject her to the kind of preparation a horse must under-take to have any chance of winning the Arc de Triomphe. He would never consider sending a horse to the post for a race of any importance unless he was satisfied it was at its best. Readers may remember how, back in her three-year-old days, Bernard had insisted on giving the mare a final gallop if she was to take her chance in the Yorkshire Oaks, an important race but a long way from the Arc. However, he was quite happy to let her run in the Cumberland Lodge in spite of her defeat in it two years before. I liked the idea, since as she really was to retire at the end of the season this would provide a possible winning finale to her racing career. The Royal race-course, where, on her first appearance she had made an indelible impression and where later she had achieved her greatest triumph would be the perfect setting for a final appearance. Furthermore, if she were to win she would then avenge her defeat in the same race two years previously.

The race was to be run on Thursday, September 24th, more than three months after Park Top's last appearance. Bernard and I were understandably worried during the days before she ran that her forelegs would not stand up to the strain of her final gallops. However, he was able to telephone me on Wednesday morning to say that all was well, and she would leave for Ascot that afternoon. Once it was certain she would run I set about studying the opposition. Until Bernard's final telephone call I had been half expecting something to go wrong and thought it would be tempting fate if I paid too much attention to the coming race.

The 1970 Cumberland Lodge saw one change in the tactics we planned for all her previous races; in this we were possibly influenced by the view expressed that the mare had lost the Coronation Cup due to the slow pace at which it had been run. Even though neither Bernard nor I accepted this explanation, we decided to run a pacemaker to assure a good gallop. We owned in partnership a useful three-year-old called Side Hill who had enough speed to do the job admirably. There were three other runners, one four-year-old and two three-year-olds. The four-year-old High Line appeared to be the greatest danger. He had won his last race, the one mile five furlong Geoffrey Freer Stakes at Newbury in the middle of August, prior to which he had been second to Prince Consort in the Princess of Wales

Stakes on the July course at Newmarket. This was close to top-class form as Prince Consort had won the Bessborough Stakes at Royal Ascot while in the previous year this Noel Murless-trained colt had been third in Intermezzo and Ribofilio in the St. Leger. High Line himself had been a good three-year-old, winning the two-mile Jockey Club Cup and had been allocated nine stone in the three-year-old Free Handicap, seven pounds below the top weight Intermezzo, and only two pounds below Caliban. The mile and a half of the Cumberland Lodge was probably too short for him, although he obviously had enough ability to show whether Park Top was still a major force in racing.

Of the three-year-olds Yellow River had a better record than Psalt, having won the two-mile Queen's Vase at Royal Ascot, but again the distance of the Cumberland Lodge was probably too short for him. Psalt, trained by George Todd, had won a maiden as a two-year-old and in his two runs in the current season the best performance had been in finishing fourth to Approval in the Dante Stakes at York in the spring. Judged by the class of horse Park Top had been racing against in her last nine races this field did not amount to much. But she had been off the race-course a long time and only the race could confirm whether Bernard's opinion that she had retained her ability was correct.

Piggott again had the mount, with Willie Carson on Side Hill. After Park Top's great exploits it might be imagined that the Cumberland Lodge, whatever its result, could only be an anti-climax to the events of 1969 and the early part of 1970. This was far from the case. The race was to be her last at Ascot and I was desperately keen for her to win it. The fact that on all known form she ought to do so, without much difficulty, made the thought of defeat all the more dismaying. She was made favourite at 5 to 4 on, with High Line 6 to 4 against, and

Yellow River at 100 to 6. The fact that she was allowed to start at nearly even money, and that High Line was well supported to beat her, showed that many regular race-goers felt she had been off the race-course for too long, or that her running in the Coronation Cup indicated she was no longer the mare she had been as a five-year-old. In her hey-day she would have been at long odds on to beat this field.

The going was officially described as firm, but firm ground at Ascot is a very different thing to firm ground at Epsom. It was a wonderful moment watching her canter back past the stands on her way to the mile and a half start, with Lester in the saddle. Memories of the King George VI and Queen Elizabeth Stakes came flooding back.

For the last time, like the matchless performer that she was, Park Top rose to the occasion magnificently. From the start Willie Carson fulfilled his role to perfection. He went straight to the front and set a really strong gallop down the hill to Swinley Bottom, pursued by High Line, Yellow River and Psalt, with Lester in his customary position at the back of the field, his behind high in the air. Willie kept Side Hill going strongly past the mile post and then right-handed up the hill, with the field racing in the same order in line ahead. Geoff Lewis on Yellow River was the first to make a move, sweeping past High Line and then overtaking Side Hill with about half a mile to run. Now Side Hill, his job done, dropped out of it. The bell rang, signalling the field was turning for home, my heart thumped and my hands shook uncontrollably. As soon as the horses were in line for home Joe Mercer on High Line challenged Yellow River and went past him. Lester moved the mare past Psalt and was still sitting still, biding his time. But despite thoughts of what had happened in this very race two years before lurking at the back of my mind, my heart began to lift. Lester was perfectly poised to annihilate the two colts in front of him if, but only if, the mare had kept her speed and her courage, and those doubtful forelegs stood the strain when the pressure was really on.

Lester appeared totally unconcerned as the field went past the quarter-mile marker. Still he did not move, no doubt watching the duel which was going on in front of him. Yellow River came back at High Line and, with a furlong to go, regained the lead. It was now or never. With a hundred and fifty yards to the post Lester at last made his move. The response was the same devastating acceleration, the burst of speed that once seen, would never be forgotten.

For the last time in her career Park Top showed that incredible speed that had so astonished Mrs. Scott when Park Top's companion had been an old pony and not high-class thoroughbred colts. With a perfectly-timed effort Park Top left her rivals standing, to pass the post with three-quarters of a length to spare over Yellow River.

Although the race was not of comparable importance or value to her great victories in earlier years, Park Top had once again asserted her authority and shown that her brilliance remained undimmed. It was a moment to savour for ever after.

Unfortunately the drama was not quite over, for as the curtain came down to tumultuous applause, the mare showed signs of the strain of her performance. As Lester began to pull her up he felt her go lame. He at once dismounted, so that she was led into the winner's enclosure without a jockey on her back, although she was once again walking sound. The sight of the riderless winner cast something of a gloom over her triumphant return, but I did not greatly care because she was back where she belonged, in the place reserved for the winner on one of the most famous race-courses in the world.

To train the mare to win this race was one of the greatest achievements in Bernard's distinguished career. To have got her in a condition to run so brilliantly he had to contend with forelegs that were clearly showing the effects of having run in twenty-two races. To have got her to stand four seasons of hard training was a feat that only a master of his trade could have achieved. This last win of Park Top's must have given Bernard, never one to show emotion, infinite satisfaction. For me, it was further proof of my luck in not only owning such a great horse but of having as my life-long friend a man whose skill as a trainer was matched only by the brilliance of the horse in his charge.

The lameness Lester felt after passing the post did not re-occur. It would have been better if it had, as then there would have been no question of her running again.

On her return to Newmarket the mare appeared to be as sound as a bell. A week went by and all was still well. Bernard then gave her a gallop and she passed this test satisfactorily. Bernard could only assume that she had knocked and injured herself, touching a nerve which made her lame momentarily, in much the same way as Remand had gone lame before the start of the Eclipse. With hindsight, our decision to give Park Top one last race at Longchamp seems inexplicable, particularly as we were both anxious the mare should retire as a winner. Clearly, to run her in the Arc would be asking too much of her, but Bernard had found a comparatively minor race for her the week following the Arc which seemed well within her grasp.

She had made a perfect farewell at Ascot and now to round off her career we wanted her to do the same on the course in the Bois de Boulogne, which was the other race-course where she had acquitted herself with such distinction.

The race was the Prix de Royallieu for fillies and mares, over one mile, five furlongs. By English standards, it was a valuable race, being worth nearly £8,000 to the winner. It looked made for the mare and Bernard was satisfied she was fit to take her chance. The fact that she did run is a perfect example of how today, good trainers do not give their horses the sort of trial they will be subjected to in a race. After Ascot Park Top was given just enough work to keep her thoroughly fit but was not asked to undertake a hard gallop. To ask a horse for the sort of effort that could be expected in a race not only taxes a horse's strength unnecessarily but, more often than not, means that the horse has given its best in the final gallop and is past its peak on the day of the race. It is the essence of skill in training to have a horse ready for a great race on that very day. The last gallop should have brought him to his peak. One gallop less and there would still be a little improvement to be made. One gallop more and the peak of condition would have been passed. Only a trainer of great knowledge and experience can be expected to produce a horse at its very best on the day when it really matters. With lesser horses, by all means gallop them to show their full potential and then have a good bet in the race following the gallop; but to win a great race a horse must be at the supreme pinnacle of fitness and at the same time fresh and not stale from being over-galloped.

I will not dwell on the unhappy events of that grey day at Longchamp. Gone was the sunshine that had always augured well for the mare. The race was to show that gone too was all the mare's sparkle.

There were six other runners, five three-year-olds and a four-year-old, Wilductrice. The latter had not run in a race of any consequence before and had not earned a rating in the French Free Handicap in the previous year. There was one English filly among the three-year-olds, Hazy Idea trained by Dick Hern. She had been a good two-year-old, winning three of her four starts, and had finished fourth to Vela in the Criterium des Pouliches in her other start. This was the race immediately before the Arc in 1969 and provided Lester with his hat-trick. As a three-year-old she had won two good races and in her last race, again in France, she had finished fourth to Sassafras in a disputed finish over a mile and seven and a half furlongs at Longchamp. Since then Sassafras had won the Arc from Nijinsky.

It is an indication of the regard with which Park Top was held that this high-class filly was given no chance of defeating the mare. The best of the French fillies appeared to be Prime Aboard, owned by Bunker Hunt. She had been fourth a few weeks earlier in the Prix Vermeille and had also been fourth in the French Oaks.

Understandably, the mare started a very hot favourite. Lester rode his usual race waiting at the back. We had no reason to feel unduly anxious as she turned into the straight with some ground to make up, for she was quite close enough to the leaders to win if she was good enough. Lester made his challenge a little earlier than on the other occasions he had ridden the mare. She made up some ground and for a few strides looked dangerous, but the brilliance had gone and for the first time in the nine races he had ridden her, she was unable to to answer his call. I saw nothing of the closing stages of the race. Once I had seen that she was not her true self and would not win I could not bear to watch. I was overwhelmed with self-reproach for allowing her to run after all she had done for me. In fact she dead-heated for third place with a filly called La Java. The race was won by Prime Abord by half a length from Hazy Idea.

Later, it was some consolation that Park Top had managed to finish equal third, as it meant that she had not been out of the first three in her last sixteen races. Since running unplaced in the Magnet Cup at York in July, 1968, as a four-year-old she had finished first twice, second once and third once; as a five-year-old, first five times and second three; and now at six she had won twice, finished second once, and third once. At the time, this tremendous record of brilliance, gameness and consistency was no consolation. I have said of racing that the tears come when one wins and not when one loses. That October day in the Bois de Boulogne came near to being the exception. As we waited for her to return to be unsaddled I was close to tears, not tears of disappointment but tears of anguish for having let the defeat happen. Luckily, the unbelievable behaviour of the French crowd saved the day. As Park Top was led in, the Longchamp race-goers began to boo. I could not believe my ears. For that crowd to boo Park Top, the mare they had taken to their hearts and from whom she had received as much, if not more,

The Sporting Life

No. 28,558   MONDAY, OCTOBER 12, 1970   One Shilling

The great mare has run her last race

PIGGOTT BOOED ON BEATEN PARK TOP

adulation than from race-goers in England, was like hearing a great prima donna being booed for faltering over one note. My anguish gave way to fury and, turning to face the crowd, I repeatedly gave them that two-fingered gesture later made famous by Harvey Smith in a much publicised incident at Hickstead. I have always been slightly jealous of him for getting the credit for bringing this singularly expressive gesture into the public eye. I feel the credit should go to me. The ever faithful Peter O'Sullevan, who had come over especially to see the mare run, duly reported the incident in his column the next morning, but more important was his headline – "The Great Mare Has Run Her Last Race".

So, her last season ended in the same way as all her

Jeers for Piggott

From TIM FITZGEORGE-PARKER : In Paris

LESTER PIGGOTT suffered the
most prolonged hostile reception I
have ever heard when he came
in after Park Top's defeat at
Longchamp yesterday.

others, in disappointment. It was far greater this time because there could be no opportunity of wiping out the memories of that miserable afternoon. Bernard minded as much
as Debo and I, and I'm sure so did Maureen. But she kept her
equanimity in a wonderful way, showing that she, like Bernard,
knew how to be a good loser as well as a good winner. I will
regret to my dying day that the mare was not retired after the
Cumberland Lodge, but it had all looked so different before the
race. I can still see the temptation of hoping to end her
career with victories on the two courses in the two countries
where she had achieved such glory and received such acclaim.
I have not been back to Longchamp and, unless I have a horse
which my trainer insists on running there, I shall not go.

The best impartial assessment of Park Top I can offer is contained in an article in the *British Racehorse* by that distinguished handicapper David Swannell. In this, which he called
"Handicapping of a Decade", he allocates weights to the best
horses of the 1960s. He gives two lists; one for three-year-olds
and one for horses of four years and upwards. Park Top, among
others, is included in both lists. In that for three-year-olds she
is well down the list and below Petite Etoile. This is clearly
right, since Petite Etoile won both the 1,000 Guineas and the
Oaks, while the mare's only major victory was in the Ribblesdale. Had she run in the Yorkshire Oaks she might have earned

a higher rating, for by the time the Vermeille came round she was past her best. In Mr. Swannell's second list the mare comes into her own. The handicap is headed by the four-year-old Exbury with ten stone, followed by Busted and Levmoss with nine stone twelve, Relko with nine stone eleven, Match III with nine stone ten pounds. Royal Palace and Park Top are bracketed together at nine stone nine. Below them are the Derby winners St. Paddy and Parthia. Petite Etoile is given nine stone six, and the only other filly in the list of sixteen is Aunt Edith, the winner of the King George VI and Queen Elizabeth Stakes in 1966, who is allotted nine stone one.

It is interesting to compare this assessment with that of the French Free Handicap for three-year-olds and upwards for 1969. The two are not directly comparable, since Mr. Swannell gives a separate list for the three-year-olds while the French handicap includes three-year-olds with the older horses.

So far as the mare is concerned, Mr. Swannell makes Levmoss three pounds her superior, a pound less than in the French handicap. I consider both figures to flatter Levmoss. Mr. Swannell rates Karabas one pound better than Park Top while the French handicap places them the other way round. Karabas won the Hardwicke as a five-year-old in 1970, but he was well beaten by Connaught in the Eclipse and finished fourth to Nijinsky, Blakeney and Crepellana in the King George VI and Queen Elizabeth Stakes, finishing five lengths behind Blakeney and a length behind Crepellana. The mare had trounced both these horses in the Arc, so it is difficult to sustain an argument that Karabas was a better horse than the mare. My view is that the mare was very considerably the better and I believe Bernard shared this view, although I doubt whether Rory and Elizabeth More O'Ferrall, Karabas's owners would agree. Anyway it is churlish to cavil – I am well satisfied that in the view of an acknowledged expert, the mare was the best of her sex in her decade. Furthermore, as well as this analytical judgement, we have heard that Lester regarded Park Top in 1969 as the best mare or filly he had ever ridden. A quotation from John Oaksey written after her defeat in the Arc sums up what the racing world felt about her that year. "It may not be fashionable to say nowadays but the English still prefer a good loser to a vainglorious winner and Park Top's tragic heroic defeat last Sunday has set the seal on her popularity. She is now without much doubt the best-loved mare since Pretty Polly and with Lester Piggott on her back, the biggest crowd-puller British flat racing has seen for many a year." What would have happened if the mare had kept well and been able to take on Nijinsky in the 1970 King George VI and Queen Elizabeth Stakes is open to conjecture. I fancy most people would argue that the outstandingly brilliant Canadian-bred and Irish-trained colt would have been a comfortable winner. I am not so sure. There are two pieces of evidence to be weighed up in trying to estimate the result of such a clash. There is the times of the respective Arc de Triomphes in which they ran. Both were narrowly defeated but whereas the colt had every chance, indeed was in front a few strides before the post, we know the mare had a desperately unlucky run. In spite of this Levmoss's time in defeating Park Top by a rapidly diminishing three-quarters of a length was .7 of a second faster than that taken by Sassafras when defeating Nijinsky by a head. The going was reckoned faster in 1969 than 1970, although not all the races on Arc day in 1969 were run in faster time than in the following year. In fairness, it should also be stated that the Canadian colt was past his best on Arc day.

Blakeney provides the second piece of evidence. He was beaten by some eight lengths by the mare in the Arc while in the following year, in the King George VI and Queen Elizabeth Stakes, Nijinsky had two lengths to spare over him at the post. However, this distance gives no indication of the supreme ease with which Nijinsky won that day. He was never out of a canter. Nevertheless, eight lengths is eight lengths and the third in the King George VI and Queen Elizabeth Stakes, Crepellana, had been many lengths behind Blakeney in the Arc. Had she kept sound, Park Top would have certainly run in the Ascot race and at the price she was likely to have started I would have had a similar bet to that which I had on her in the Arc. What I would have felt like during the days and hours preceding the race I can imagine only too easily, so perhaps it was just as well she was not in the field. Blakeney is only one of a number of colts who the mare raced against who have been quick to make their name as stallions. Blakeney himself has already sired the winner of the English and Irish Oaks Juliet Marnie, and other good winners, while Wolver Hollow is the sire of Wollow, beaten favourite of the 1976 Derby. Prince Regent, Candy Cane and Connaught have all made their mark with their first two crops, and this is perhaps further evidence of the class of colt the mare had to contend with in her racing days.

The Park Top story is not yet over. After that dreadful day in the Bois she went into well-deserved retirement. Unfortunately, her stud career has been bedevilled by misfortune, thus allowing the wiseacres to shake their heads and say : "There, that is what happens if you are greedy and keep a mare in training until she is six." This is an argument that does not stand up to the facts. Secretariat's dam ran more than 30 times and she was only one example of the many top-class American horses that have been bred from mares who saw the race-course on a great many more occasions than Park Top's twenty-four appearances.

Her first mating was with Tudor Melody. She was in foal after her first covering. Unfortunately, the resulting foal was born more than two months prematurely. The filly was tiny, with a twisted off-hind leg. Had she been a colt it would have probably been put down at once. Since she was a filly, she was reared, but while the hind leg gradually straightened, she never overcame the handicap of her early birth. As she got older, she became increasingly like a miniature of her mother, the same colour, the same star on her forehead and the same sweet temperament. As it turned out later, she also inherited some of the mare's indomitable courage. Although little more than 14 hands she went into training at Stanley House where she was put in Maureen's charge. Had she only been a few inches taller she might well have made a name for herself on the race-course. I named her Willow Song. Students of Shakespeare will recall that this is the name of the song Desdemona sings just before she is murdered by Othello. Since Shakespeare was a Tudor playwright this song qualifies as a Tudor melody, while Park Top is a green sward on the moors in Yorkshire. The name seemed appropriate, as well as being worthy of Park Top's daughter.

The record books will show that Willow Song's best performance in the four starts she had as a two-year-old, her only season to race, was a second in a modest maiden at Nottingham. Considering that she measured 14 hands 3 inches that afternoon, it was a fine performance. She showed immense courage and gave all she had.

She showed the same determination in her last outing when fourth in a big field at Lingfield, where but for the clinging mud she might have won. Except in the matter of size she had grown more and more like her dam. Bernard used to say that sometimes on misty mornings on the heath, watching the little filly work was like seeing a miniature ghost of the great mare go swinging past. She was not covered at three to give her more time to grow and mature. This year she is to be covered by Sharpen Up.

Park Top was next sent to Roan Rocket, only to slip twins. Paul Mellon with great generosity immediately agreed to my request to send her to Mill Reef. Great was our joy when she was tested in foal to the great American Derby and Arc de Triomphe winner. Alas, once again she slipped. With such a record it seemed unwise to send her yet again to an expensive stallion so she was sent to Sharpen Up. This horse had been a very fast two-year-old when trained by Bernard, ending up a highly successful first season by taking the Middle Park at Newmarket. For the first time she did not get in foal. She returned to the same horse in 1975 and was got in foal.

All appeared to be going well with the mare until the first week in February, 1976, when she apparently picked up an infection. She developed a high temperature and there was a lot of swelling in her hind legs. For a day or two, Mr. Evans, the Stud Groom at Sidehill, and the vet feared for her life and that of the unborn foal. After four days she gave birth to a filly, three weeks prematurely. The mare quickly recovered but the foal, although well made and of average size, continues to give cause for some concern. All may yet be well and the little filly is a far better foal than was Willow Song.

The secret of Park Top's brilliance was the combination of her sire's stamina coupled with the tremendous speed that lay in her dam's pedigree. Provided she remains well I shall try and reproduce this combination only in reverse. The mare stayed at least one mile five furlongs and I shall continue to send her to top-class sprinters so that there is little danger of the offspring lacking speed. She can be relied upon to provide the stamina.

Whatever the future holds for the mare, for Willow Song, or the new foal, one thing is certain as far as I'm concerned: there will never be a race-horse like Park Top. At the end of her story, though, I cannot claim with Edith Piaf that "Je ne regrette rien". I have a number of regrets. Running the mare in that last race at Longchamp, and to a lesser extent letting her take her chance in the Champion, are perhaps the chief of them. I am, of course, sorry that she did not win the Arc or a second Coronation Cup, but more than these defeats I mind her losing, through no fault of her own, the Eclipse. No mare or filly has ever won this great event. For her to have been the first of her sex to win the world famous Sandown race would have been wholly appropriate.

Coda

It is now thirty years since the triumphs of Park Top as a five-year-old, but my memory of them is as vivid as the day they took place. Although to non-racing people this may seem trivial, owning Park Top was one of the great emotional experiences of my life. The love of racing that had long remained dormant in my family was with me from my earliest schooldays. I bought my first horse in 1947 but had to wait many years before I had a winner of any kind. Then, to own a race mare who would find her place in the racing history of this century was beyond my wildest dreams. Now, her achievements are a constant source of happy recollections.

Park Top's career covered the whole gamut of the sport. There were triumphs (the King George and Queen Elizabeth, the Hardwicke and the Ribblesdale at Ascot) and disappointments (the Arc, the Eclipse and the Champion Stakes), but that, to coin a tired phrase, is racing. She lived on in retirement at Buttermilk Stud and died peacefully at the age of twenty-five. After her death I was touched to receive many letters of condolence, including some from America.

Finally, I would like to remind readers that she was trained by my great friend Bernard van Cutsem while he was suffering from the cancer which sadly brought his life to an all too early end.

Appendix
Raceform 1967-70

1967
WINDSOR, MAY 22nd

MAR LODGE PLATE (3-Y-O) £345   1m 2f

PARK TOP 8-7 Maddock (1) *gd sort; lw; hdwy 4f out; led over 1f out; easily* ...   .   —1

Lord Sing 8-10 Piggott (2) *led over 1m; no imp*   ...   1½.2

Court Gem 8-7 Durr (12) *3rd st; ev ch over 1f out; unable qckn* nk.3

Red Hugh 8-10 R. Hutchinson (10) *4th st; ev ch 2f out; one pce fnl f* ¾.4

Orcharine 8-2‡⁵ A. Murray (5) *5th st; no hdwy fnl 2f*   ...   15.5

Nine One 8-10 Eldin (6) *2nd st; wknd wl over 2f out*   ...   ½.6

Flying Barnie 8-10 Barclay (9) *6th st; no hdwy*   ...   ...   o

Time to Go 8-7 Greening (8) *w'like; neat* ...   .   o

Lower Slaughter 8-7 Stringer (3) *unf; dwlt s*   ...   ...   o

Khyly-Khub 8-0‡⁷ Ginn (4) *bkwd*   ...   .   o

Parthian Fare 8-3‡⁷ M. Lee (11) *w'like; a.bhd*   ...   ...   o

Also ran: Saucy Councillor 8-2‡⁵ Sexton (14); Historical 8-7 Cook (13); Gay Norwegian 8-10 Ryan (7).

S.P.: 5/2 Court Gem (tchd 3/1), 5 PARK TOP (6/1—9/2), 11/2 Lord Sing (4/1—6/1); Nine One (tchd 6/1, blow); 10 Red Hugh (op 7/1); Flying Barnie (op 100/8); Saucy Councillor (op 8/1); 25 Ors.

Tote—39/10; 11/4, 6/4, 6/4.   14 Rn.   2m 19.6.

NEWBURY, JUNE 14th
TWYFORD STAKES (3-Y-O F) £409 8s.   1m 2f

Park Top 8-10 Maddock (2) *lw; 5th st; led 2f out; edgd lft;
easily* ... ... —1

Caramel 8-5 G. Lewis (3) *2nd st; ev ch whn squeezd for rm
2f out; one pce* 4.2

Raheema 8-5 Mercer (4) *h; led 1m; wknd 1f out* 2.3

Cathey III 8-10 G. Moore (5) *lw; 3rd st; ev ch when squeezd
out 2f out; nt rcvr* hd.4

Precious Light 8-5 Breasley (1) *lw; 4th st; no hdwy fnl 2f* ... 1.5

S.P.: 10/11 Cathey III (op. 11/8), 2 Park Top (6/4—9/4), 8 Caramel
(firm), Precious Light (op 7/1), 33 Raheema.

Tote—22/6 (102/10).   5 Rn.   2m 11.1

ROYAL ASCOT, JUNE 21st
RIBBLESDALE STAKES (3-Y-O F) £4606 10s.   1m 4f

Park Top 8-10 Maddock *5th st; led over 1f out; smoothly* ... —1

St. Pauli Girl 8-10 Raymond *lw; 3rd st; led 2f out; r.o wl* ... ½.2

Plotina 8-10 G. Moore *4th st; ev ch 2f out; unable qckn* ... 2.3

Soon Parted 8-6 Eldin *gd hdwy fnl 2f r.o* 3.4

The Nun 8-10 Mercer *6th st; no hdwy fnl 2f* ¾.5

Shamrock's Beauty 8-6 Keith *lost pl over 3f out; no ch fnl 2f* 3.6

Mary Charlotte 8-10 Lake *led over 5f out; led over 3f out;
wknd wl over 1f out* ½.7

Silk II 8-6 Breasley *lw; led over 6f; led over 4f out; 2nd st;
wknd 2f out* ... ... o

Village 8-6 W. Williamson *dwlt s* ... ... o

Also ran: Avadera 8-6 D. Smith (lw), Westerlands Athene 8-6 Barclay, Meyerling 8-6 R. Hutchinson.

S.P.: 6/4 St. Pauli Girl (tchd 2/1), 9/2 Park Top (4/1—5/1), 11/2
Plotina (op 5/1), 13/2 Silk II (op 8/1), 15/2 The Nun (8/1—7/1),
100/7 Mary Charlotte, Avadera, 25 Ors.

Tote—30/2; 9/-, 5/8, 8/4.   12 Rn.   2m 35.65.

BRIGHTON CUP (H'CAP) £2227   abt 1m 4f

PARK TOP 3-8-2 Maddock *lw; 4th st; led ins fnl f; rn green; comf* ... ... —1

Happy Haven 5-7-12 R. Hutchinson *5th st; led wl over 1f out; r.o wl* ... ... $1\frac{1}{2}$.2

Grock II 4-7-3 Cullen *3rd st; ev ch 2f out; one pce* 2.3

Ginger Boy 3-6-10(^{1})‡^{7} Errington *swtg; led over 5f out; wknd over 1f out* ... ... $\frac{1}{2}$.4

Royal Rubicon 5-8-10 Breasley *gd hdwy fnl 2f; nvr nr to chall* 3.5

Italiano 4-7-1‡^{7} Stott *lw; late hdwy; nvr nrr* nk.6

Beauatire 5-6-13‡^{5} Dicey *led over 6f; 2nd st; wknd over 2f out* 0

Nous Esperons 4-7-8 M. Thomas *prom over 7f* 0

Santaway 8-7-7 T. Carter *lw; 6th st; wknd 2f out* 0

Manchu 4-7-2(^{2}) Reader *prom 6f; t.o fnl 4f* 0

Cabouchon 6-6-7‡^{7} Lemon *h; prom 7f; t.o fnl 4f* 0

Le Garcon 6-7-12 D. W. Morris *a.bhd; t.o fnl 4f* 0

S.P.: 6/4 PARK TOP (7/4—5/4), 8 Royal Rubicon (op 7/1); Santaway (op 7/1), 100/8 Le Garcon (op 8/1), Happy Haven (op 10/1), Italiano (op 10/1), Nous Esperons (tchd 100/7), 100/7 Grock II, Ginger Boy, 33 Beauatire, 50 Ors.

Tote—9/-; 5/6, 9/4, 25/6.   12 Rn.   No time taken.

PRIX VERMEILLE (3-Y-O F) £41,633 10S.   1m 4f

Casaque Grise 9-2 Y. Saint-Martin	...	...	...	—1
Percale 9-2 J. Deforge ...	...	...	...	1.2
Heath Rose 9-2 J Taillard	...	...	...	s.nk.3
Iskereen 9-2 L. Ward ...	...	...	...	3.4
Modeste 9-2 L. Flavien	...	...	...	¾.5
Armoricana 9-2 V. Dupays	...	...	...	4.6
Astuce 9-2 H. Samanl ...	...	...	...	o
Pink Gem 9-2 G. Moore	...	...	...	o
Cranberry Sauce 9-2 A. Barclay ...	...	...	...	o
Park Top 9-2 R. Maddock	...	...	...	o
Serenitas 9-2 G. Thiboeuf	...	...	...	o
Tidra 9-2 F. Head	...	...	...	o
Reginskaia 9-2 J. C. Desaint	...	...	...	o
Lady Aureola 9-2 R. Jallu	...	...	...	o
Gazala 9-2 M. Philipperon	...	...	...	o
Gorda 9-2 W. Pyers ...	...	...	...	o
Pro Arte 9-2 M. Depalmas	...	...	...	o
Ingrette 9-2 R. Poincelet	...	...	...	o
Arawak 9-2 W. Williamson	...	...	...	o

19 Rn.   2m 43.7

NEWMARKET, APRIL 30th

TOTALISATOR SPRING HANDICAP   1m (R.M.)
£5956 10s. (£1750; £855; £228 10s.)

GOLDEN MEAN 5-8-2 Durr (9) *led wl over 1f out; easily*   ...   —1

Waterloo Place 4-8-9 Mercer (8) *wl bhd 5f; gd hdwy 2f out; ev
ch 1f out; unable qckn* 4.2

Owen Anthony 4-7-3‡[5] (8x) R. Dicey (13) *hdwy over 2f out;
ev ch over 1f out; one pce fnl f* 1½.3

William of Orange 4-6-10‡[7] Enright (5) *ev ch 2f out; wknd 1f
out* 2.4

Chapman's Peak 4-7-1([8])‡[7] Duffield (2) *late hdwy; nvr nr to
chall* s.h.5

Hang On 4-8-0 Barclay (12) *ev ch 2f out; wknd wl over 1f out*   1.6

Shady Knight 5-7-6 ([3])‡[3] A. Murray (4) *gd spd 6f* 1½.7

Park Top 4-9-5 Maddock (16) *ev ch 2f out; r.o one pce*   ...1½.8

Sammy Denoun 4-7-0 Parkes (18) *lw; h; prom 6f*   0

Norton Priory 5-7-13 Bentley (20) *prom 4f*   0

Dale Cross 4-7-12 E. Johnson (6) *lw; prom 5f*   0

Blazing Scent 9-7-2‡[5] Still (3) *swtg; stdy hdwy fnl 2f; r.o*   ...   0

Ward Drill 6-7-6 T. Carter (7) *h; led over 6f*   0

Off the Hook 6-8-2 Jago (11) *outpcd*   0

Good Match 4-8-6 Breasley (1) *lw; bhd fnl 3f*   0

Also ran: Persian Empire 5-8-12 Piggott (15), Ben Nevus 6-8-7 E. Hide
(10), Come April 4-8-2 G. Lewis (19), Starboard Watch 4-7-13 R.
Hutchinson (17), Cumshaw 7-7-12([1]) Tulk (21), Danella 6-7-11 P. Robinson (14).

S.P.: 100/30 Park Top (op 5/1), 8 Waterloo Place (tchd 10/1),
9 Owen Anthony (7/1—10/1), 100/9 Persian Empire (tchd 100/8),
Shady Knight (op 100/6, blow), 100/8 Hang On (op 100/7, blow),
Cumshaw (tchd 100/7), 100/6 Ben Nevus (tchd 20/1), Come April
(op 100/7), Blazing Scent (20/1—100/7), 20 GOLDEN MEAN, Good
Match, Dale Cross, Danella, Sammy Denoun, 25 Ors.

Tote—137/-; 31/2, 9/10, 10/8.   21 Rn.   1m 40.54.

ORMONDE STAKES £1108 (£306; £145 10s.)   1m 5f 75y

HOPEFUL VENTURE 4-8-12 Barclay *lw; mde most; drew clr fnl f* ...   . —1

Park Top 4-8-9 Maddock *3rd tl 6f out; sn disp ld tl 2nd st; sn btn* 5.2

Starry Halo 4-8-12 Durr *lw; 2nd tl 3rd 6f out; sn no ch* ... 10.3

S.P.: Evens HOPEFUL VENTURE (tchd 10/11), 13/8 Park Top (op 11/10); 11/2 Starry Halo (tchd 7/1).

Tote—7/- (10/2).   3 Rn.   3m 9.7

MAGNET CUP (H'CAP) £3822 9s. (£1127: £553 10s.: £152 1s.)
1m 2f 110y

FARM WALK 6-8-13 Seagrave *lw; last st; good hdwy to ld bel dist; r.o wl* ...   . —1

Castle Yard 5-8-3 Williamson *7th st; w wnr bel dist; one pce* 2.2

Private Room 4-7-13 M. Thomas *lw; h; wnt 2nd st; sn led & wnt clr; hdd bel dist; nt r.o* ½.3

Le Garcon 7-7-11 W. Carson *8th st; r.o und press fnl 3f* ... 2.4

Park Top 4-9-4 Maddock *9th st; effrt 3f out; ch whn hng lft bel dist; sn btn* nk.5

Big Hat 3-7-3‡[7] Clarkson *lw; h; prom tl 6th st; no hdwy* ... 2.6

Polymint 8-7-7‡[7] Enright *b; h; led to st; sn hdd & btn* ... 0

Game All 4-8-12 Piggott *cl up tl 3rd st; efft 2f out; sn btn* ... 0

Straight King 5-8-8 Etherington *lw; cl up; 4th st; wknd 2f out* 0

Pertinacity 4-9-0 Swinburn *prom; 5th st; btn 3f out* ... 0

S.P.: 3 Park Top (op 5/1), 100/3 Game All (op 5/2), 7 Big Hat (tchd 10/1), 8 FARM WALK (tchd 9/1), Castle Yard (op 7/1), 9 Pertinacity (firm), 10 Le Garcon (tchd 100/8), 20 Private Room (tchd 100/6), 25 Polymint, 33 Straight King.

Tote—26/8; 20/6, 9/10, 19/4.   10 Rn.   2m 14.2.

BRIGHTON, AUGUST 7th

BRIGHTON CHALLENGE CUP £1512 (£394: £194) abt 1m 4f
(H'CAP)

PARK TOP 4-9-10 G. Lewis *lw; 3rd st; led over 1f out; r.o wl* ... —1

Santaway 9-8-0(²)‡⁵ Hayward *led over 4f out; unable qckn fnl f* 1½.2

Lexicon 4-8-12‡³ D. Maitland *4th st; one pce fnl f* 6.3

Merkades 3-7-11 B. Jago *h; 2nd st; wknd 2f out* 6.4

Beauatire 6-8-1 Dingwall *5th st; no hdwy fnl 3f* 6.5

Resistance 6-8-10‡⁷ Haines *6th st; nvr nr to chall* 3.6

Golden Bolt 5-7-11‡⁷ Holley *t.o fnl 4f* ... ... o

Also ran: Happy Haven 6-8-8 J. Wilson, Duke Street 6-7-11‡³ (6x) R. Dicey.

S.P.: 2 PARK TOP (op 3/1), Santaway (tchd 7/4), 8 Lexicon (tchd 10/1), 10 Merkades (op 8/1), Resistance (op 8/1), 100/8 Happy Haven (op 10/1), 100/7 Duke Street, 100/6 Beauatire, 33 Golden Bolt.

Tote—17/-; 6/-, 5/4, 7/10 (D: 18/4). 9 Rn. 2m 32 (flag).

NEWBURY, AUGUST 17th

OXFORDSHIRE STAKES £3547 16s. (£1038 : £504 : £130 4s.)
1m 5f 60y

LEVMOSS 3-8-4(¹) B. Taylor *lw; 5th st; str rn fnl f; led last strides*   —1

Canterbury 3-8-3 Williamson *w'like; scope; 4th st; led 3f out r.o wl* nk.2

Park Top 4-9-3 G. Lewis *lw; 6th st; ev ch fnl 2f; unable qckn cl hme* hd.3

Dancing Moss 4-9-3 Barclay *2nd st; wknd over 1f out; bttr for r* 6.4

Fortissimo 4-9-3 Boothman *3rd st; ev ch 3f out; wknd 2f out* 2.5

Mount Athos 3-8-9 R. Hutchinson *lw; 7th st; drvn over 2f out; no rspnse* nk.6

Young Alexander 3-8-3 Elliott *led tl 3f out* 0

St. Patrick's Blue 3-8-3 Mercer *a.bhd; last st* 0

March Parade 6-9-0 Raymond *lw; 8th st; t.o* 0

Easter Island 6-9-0 Moss *bkwd; dwlt s; 9th st; t.o* 0

S.P.: 2 Mount Athos (7/4—9/4), 3 Park Top (tchd 11/4), 7/2 Canterbury (op 9/2), 100/8 Fortissimo (op 10/1), 100/6 LEVMOSS, Dancing Moss, 20 St. Patrick's Blue, 33 Ors.

Tote—62/8; 19/-, 8/-, 10/2.   10 Rn.   3m 2.4.

LONGCHAMP, SEPT. 8th

PRIX D'HEDOUVILLE £6087 15s.   1m 3f 110y

PARK TOP 4-9-1 G. Lewis ... ... —1

Beau Paon 4-9-6 Y. Saint-Martin 1½.2

Bagdad 4-9-6 J. Deforge s.h.3

Tiber 4-9-4 L. Piggott (h) ½.4

Right Honourable 3-8-9 W. Pyers 1½.5

Jamaico 4-9-2 F. Head ¾.6

11 Rn.   2m 32.4.

ASCOT, SEPTEMBER 26th

CUMBERLAND LODGE STAKES £2418 (£570 : £270)   1m 4f

CHICAGO 4-8-11 R. Hutchinson *lw; 3rd st; pulld out 1f out; qcknd & led ins fnl f; r.o*   ...   .   —1

Park Top 4-9-0 G. Lewis *4th st; led wl over 1f out; wknd ins. fnl f* 4.2

Tiber 4-9-0 Piggott *lw; h; hrd drvn 4f out; 5th st; nvr nrr* ...   5.3

Noblesse Oblige 3-7-11 Barclay *h; 2nd st; led 2f out; one pce* ...   ½.4

Midnight Marauder 6-8-11 Mercer *swtg; led 10f* 8.5

S.P.: 7/4 Park Top (15/8—13/8), 5/2 CHICAGO (op 2/1), Tiber (op 4/1, blow), 8 Noblesse Oblige (tchd 10/1), 100/7 Midnight Marauder.

Tote—13/- (40/2)   5 Rn.   Unofficial time 2m 47.8.

1969
LONGCHAMP, MAY 22nd

PRIX DE LA SEINE (F AND M) £2602   1m 4f

PARK TOP 5-8-13 L. Piggott	...	...	...	... —1
Pandora Bay 4-8-13 G. Thiboeuf		...	...	... 2½.2
Blanca 4-8-7 J. Massard	...	...	...	... ½.3
Egeenne 4-8-7 Y. Saint-Martin	...	...	...	... 1½.4
Djeva 7-8-2‡[4] S Kessas	...	...	...	... nk.5
Tenace 6-8-7 L. Flavien	...	...	...	... 1½.6

8 Rn.   2m 41.5.

EPSOM, JUNE 5th

CORONATION CUP £11,457 6s. (£3378 : £1659 : £455 14s.)
(C AND F)   1m 4f

PARK TOP 5-9-0 Piggott *2nd st; led ins fnl f; clevly* ...   ...   —1

Mount Athos 4-9-0 R. Hutchinson *lw; 4th st; ev ch fnl f; r.o wl*   ¾.2

Connaught 4-9-0 Barclay *lw; led over 7f out; hrd drvn over 1f*
out; one pce 1½.3

Remand 4-9-0 Mercer, *rdn 5f out; 3 st; wknd 3f out*   ...   6.4

Crozier 6-9-3 Keith *lw; h; dwlt s; nvr nrr* 2.5

Val d'Aoste 4-9-0 G. Lewis *gd sort; 5th st; wknd 3f out*   ...   ½.6

Hipster 5-9-3 Lindley *lw; led over 4f; 6th st; t.o fnl 3f*   ...   7

Ribero (100/9) withdrawn; not under orders

S.P.: 9/4 Remand (tchd 7/2), 11/4 PARK TOP (op 3/1), Connaught,
100/7 Crozier (firm), Mount Athos (op 100/8), 20 Val d'Aoste, 50
Hipster.

Tote—15/2; 7/6, 13/8, 5/10 (D. 128/2).   7 Rn.   2m 37.48.

ASCOT, JUNE 20th

HARDWICKE STAKES (C AND F)   1m 4f
£9256 13s (£2679 : £1279 10s. : £299 17s.)

PARK TOP 5-8-9 G. Lewis *lw; hld up; 2nd st; qcknd & led wl ins*
fnl f ...   .   —1

Chicago 5-8-12 R. Hutchinson *lw; led; qcknd 7f out; r.o wl* ... 1½.2

Bringley 4-8-5 B. Taylor *4th st; hdwy 2f out; nvr nrr*   ... 1½.3

Rangong 4-8-8 Barclay *lw; 3rd st; ev ch 1f out; unable qckn*   ¾.4

S.P.: 11/8 PARK TOP (op 11/10), 2 Chicago (tchd 13/8), 3 Rangong
(op 7/2), 25 Bringley.

Tote—8/8 (19/-).   4 Rn   2m 59.01.

SANDOWN, JULY 5th

ECLIPSE STAKES £25,829 5s. (£7605 : £3727 10s. : £1013 5s.)   1m 2f
(C AND F)

WOLVER HOLLOW 5-9-5 Piggott (2) *swtg; s.s; stdy hdwy on ins
3f out; led 1f out; r.o wl* ...   . —1

Park Top 5-9-2 G. Lewis (8) *lw; 4th st; chckd & chngd psn over
2f out; hrd drvn wl over 1f out; ev ch ins fnl f; unable
qckn* 2½.2

Hogarth (ITY) 4-9-5 C. Ferrari (4) *str; cmpt; lw; 2nd st; led wl
over 1f out; one pce fnl f* 3.3

Timmy My Boy 4-9-5 Barclay (1) *gd sort; lw; 6th st; ev ch 2f
out; wknd fnl f* 1.4

Rocked 3-8-7 W. Williamson (3) *lw; led over 8f* 2.5

Light Wind II 4-9-5 Swinburn (6) *gd sort; lw; 5th st; nvr nr to
chl* 2.6

Royal Rocket 4-9-5 Durr (5) *swtg; 3rd st; wknd wl over 2f out* hd.7

Remand (8/1) withdrawn; not under orders (Rule 4 applies)

S.P. : 4/5 Park Top (10/11—8/11), 13/2 Timmy My Boy (tchd 7/1),
8 WOLVER HOLLOW (op 100/8, blow), 9 Light Wind II (tchd 10/1,
blow), 100/7 Royal Rocket (op 25/1, blow), 100/6 Rocked, 33
Hogarth.

Tote—21/-; 5/10, 4/6, 14/- (D : 16/10).   7 Rn.   2m 12.1.

ASCOT, JULY 26th

KING GEORGE VI AND QUEEN ELIZABETH STAKES (C AND F)
£31,122 10s. (£9150 : £4475 : £1202 10s.)   1m 4f

Park Top 5-9-4 Piggott *in rear 3f out; rapid hdwy on ins over
2f out; led over 1f out; comf*   ...   . —1

Crozier 6-9-7 Keith *lw; h; 5th st; led wl over 1f out; r.o wl* ... 1½.2

Hogarth (ITY) 4-9-7 C. Ferrari *4th st; ev ch fnl f; r.o*   ... nk.3

Felicio II 4-9-7 W. Pyers *lw; h; dwlt s; wl bhd 9f; gd hdwy 2f
out; unable qckn fnl f* 3.4

Speed Symboli (JAP) 6-9-7 Y. Nohira *w'like lw; 2nd st; led over
2f out; one pce* 4.5

Timmy My Boy 4-9-7 Barclay *h; 3rd st; ev ch 2f out; wknd
over 1f out* 3.6

Soyeux (FR) 4-9-7 R. Poincelet *nvr nrr* 2½.7

Chicago 5-9-7 R. Hutchinson *lw 6th st; wknd over 2f out*   ... 3.8

Coolroy 8-9-7 Starkey *led over 9f*   9

S.P.: 9/4 Park Top (op 7/4), Felicio II (op 11/4), 6 Timmy My Boy
(tchd 13/2), 8 Chicago (op 7/1), 10 Soyeux (8/1—100/9), 20 Hogarth, 25 Speed Symboli, 28 Crozier, 150 Coolroy.

Tote—10/-; 5/8, 14/10, 21/8 (D: 90/10).   9 Rn.   2m 32.46.

LONGCHAMP, SEPTEMBER 7th

PRIX FOY £7689 10s.   1m 3f

Park Top 5-9-1 L. Piggott	...	...	...	... —1
Felicio 4-9-4 W. Pyers (h)	...	...	...	... 2.2
Pandora Bay 4-8-13 G. Thiboeuf	...	...	...	... 1.3
Danoso 4-8-12 R. Poincelet	...	...	...	... 2.4
Baghdad 5-9-4 G. Lewis	...	...	...	... 5.5
Scherzo 4-8-12 G. Rivases	...	...	...	... 1.6

8 Rn.   2m 19.8.

LONGCHAMP, OCTOBER 5th

PRIX DE L'ARC TRIOMPHE (C AND F) £88,810   1m 4f

LEVMOSS 4-9-6 W. Williamson *a.prom; led ent st; rdn clr over 1f out; r.o wl* ...   .   —1

Park Top 5-9-3 L. Piggott *hld up; pulld outsde 2f out; str run fr bel dist; nt rch wnr* ¾.2

Grandier 5-9-6 M. Philipperon *hdwy & ev ch 2f out; r.o*   ...   3.3

Candy Cane 4-9-6 G. Thiboeuf *hdwy over 2f out; sn rdn; unable qckn* 1.4

Prince Regent 3-8-10 G. Lewis *hld up; hdwy & nt cir rn over 2f out; not qckn fnl f* s.h.5

Chaparral 3-8-10 F. Head *2nd st; chall over 2f out; one pce* ...   nk.6

Remand 4-9-6 J. Mercer *a.prom; 6th st; r.o one pce* 2½.7

Belbury 3-8-10 H. Samani *nvr nrr* nk.8

Blakeney 3-8-10 E. Johnson *led to ½ way; no ch fnl 3f*   ... s.nk.9

Zbor 4-9-6 A. Zekachev *late hdwy; fin wl* ½.10

Bonconte di Montefeltro 3-8-10 B. Agriformi *led ½ way tl 3rd st; sn wknd*   ...   .   o

Shoemaker 3-8-10 D. Keith *hdwy ½ wy; 4th st; sn wknd*   ...   o

Ribofilio 3-8-10 R. Hutchinson *pulld hrd; in tch to ½ wy; n.d aftr*   ...   .   o

Goodley 3-8-10 A. Barclay *wnt 5th & drvn st; sn no ch*   ...   o

Saraca 3-8-7 Y. Saint-Martin *prom tl wknd appr st; t.o*   ...   o

Also ran: Fiasco 7-9-6 A. Klimscha; Copsale 6-9-6 J. Lindley (h); Speed Symboli (JAP) 6-9-6 Y. Nohira; Carmarthen 5-9-6 J. L. Durry; Roseliere 4-9-3 Y. Josse; Djakao 3-8-10 J. Deforge; Beaugency 3-8-10 J. Taillard; Yelapa 3-8-10 W. Pyers; Crepellana 3-8-7 R. Poincelet.

24 Rn.   2m 29.

CHAMPION STAKES £25,112 2s. (£7426 : £3663 : £1028 18s.)
(C AND F)   1m 2f (A.F.)

FLOSSY (FR) 3-8-4 J. Deforge (1) *w'like; scope; h; led wl over 1f out; qcknd; drvn out* ...   .   —1

Park Top 5-8-11 L. Piggott (7) *lw; ev ch 2f out; hrd drvn over 1f out; no imp* 2.2

Lorenzaccio 4-9-0 Y. Saint-Martin (5) *hdwy fnl f; nvr nrr*   ...   4.3

Hogarth (ITY) 4-9-0 C. Ferrari (2) *lw; ev ch 2f out; r.o one pce*   3.4

Locris 5-9-0 R. Poincelet (9) *hdwy over 1f out; nvr nr to chall* nk.5

Connaught 4-9-0 A. Barclay (6) *in ld over 8f out; wknd over 1f out* 2½.6

Shoemaker 3-8-7 D. Keith (8) *ev ch 2f out; wknd over 1f out* ...   o

Principal Boy 4-9-0 G. Lewis (10) *ev ch 2f out; wknd wl over 1f out* ...   .   o

Hecuba 3-8-4 W. Williamson (4) *lw; outpcd*   ...   ...   o

S.P.: 40/85 Park Top (tchd 8/11), 6 Connaught (tchd 5/1), 100/9 Locris (tchd 100/7), 100/7 FLOSSY (op 20/1), Shoemaker (op 10/1), 20 Lorenzaccio (op 100/7), 25 Ors.

Tote—83/6 : 19/8 : 5/- : 12/- (D. 102/8).   9 Rn.   2m 8.06.

1970

LONGCHAMP, MAY 7th

LA COUPE £6115 10s.   1m 5f

PARK TOP 6-9-1 L. Piggott   ...   .   —1
Chaparral 4-9-4 F. Head ½.2
Le Chouan 4-9-4 Y. Saint-Martin ½.3
Soyeux 5-9-4 S. Leonardos 5.4

4 Rn.   2m 49.5.

EPSOM, JUNE 4th

Wind: Strong half behind.

CORONATION CUP £11,430 10s. (£3370: £1655)   1m 4f

CALIBAN 4-9-0 A. Barclay *lw; made all; qcknd over 1f out; r.o wl* ...   .   —1

Park Top (fav) 6-9-0 L. Piggott *lw; 3rd st; shken up 2f out str run fnl f; too much to do* ¾.2

Shoemaker 4-9-0 D. Keith *lw; 4th st; ev ch 2f out; one pce ins fnl f* ¾.3

Swallow Tail II (H) 5-9-3 A. Murray *2nd st; wknd 2f out*   ...   5.4

S.P.: 4/11 Park Top (from 1/2), 9/2 Shoemaker (op 3/1), 8 CALIBAN (tchd 10/1), 25 Swallow Tail II.

Tote—53/6 F 58/6.   4 Rn.   2m 49.20.

ASCOT, SEPTEMBER 24th

CUMBERLAND LODGE STAKES £2999 4s. (£867 4s.: £413 12s.)   1m 4f

PARK TOP (fav) 6-9-4 L. Piggott *b; 4th st; led wl ins fnl f smoothly; lame nr fore after race*   ...   .   —1

Yellow River 3-8-3 G. Lewis *led over 4f out; led ins fnl f; r.o wl*   ¾.2

High Line 4-9-0 J. Mercer *swtg; 2nd st; led 2f out; unable qckn fnl f* 1.3

Psalt (H) 3-8-0 F. Durr *5th st; no hdwy fnl 2f* 7.4

Side Hill 3-8-0 W. Carson *led over 7f* 15.5

S.P.: 4/5 PARK TOP (tchd 8/11), 6/4 High Line, 100/6 Yellow River (from 20/1), 20/1 Psalt (early 100/8), 50/1 Side Hill.

Tote—6/6 F 31/-.   5 Rn.   2m 33.5.

LONGCHAMP, OCTOBER 11th

PRIX DE ROYALLIEU (F AND M) £7780 5s.   1m 5f

PRIME ABORD 3-8-7 M. Philipperon	...	...	...	—1
Hazy Idea 3-8-5 J. Mercer	...	...	...	½.2
Park Top 6-9-2 L. Piggott	...	...	...	d.h.3
La Java 3-8-5 A Gibert	...	...	...	d.h.3
Peronelle (FR) 3-8-9 B. Taylor ...	...	...	...	¾.5
Wilductrice 4-8-13 Y. Saint-Martin	...	...	...	8.6

7 Rn.   2m 53.7.

THE RACING RECORD OF PARK TOP

Did not run

1966 — Two Years

Did not run

1967 — Three Years

Race	Course	Distance	Ran	Odds	Result	Beaten	Value
Mar Lodge Plate	Windsor	1¼ m.	14 ran	5–1	WON	1½ l.	345
Twyford Stakes	Newbury	1¼ m.	5 ran	2–1	WON	4 l.	409
Ribblesdale Stakes	Ascot	1½ m.	12 ran	9–2	WON	½ l.	4,607
Brighton Cup	Brighton	1½ m.	12 ran	6–4	WON	1½ l.	2,227
Prix Vermeille	Longchamp	1½ m.	19 ran	10–1	Unpl.	—	—

1968 — Four Years

Race	Course	Distance	Ran	Odds	Result	Beaten	Value
Totalisator Spring Handicap	Newmarket	1 m.	21 ran	10–3	Unpl.	—	—
Ormonde Stakes	Chester	1⅝ m.	3 ran	13–8	2nd	5 l.	306
Magnet Cup	York	1¼ m.	10 ran	3–1	Unpl.	—	—
Challenge Cup	Brighton	1½ m.	9 ran	2–1	WON	1½ l.	1,512
Oxfordshire Stakes	Newbury	1⅝ m.	10 ran	3–1	3rd	nk., hd.	504
Prix d'Hedouville	Longchamp	1⅜ m.	11 ran	6–1	WON	1½ l.	6,078
Cumberland Lodge Stakes	Ascot	1½ m.	5 ran	7–4	2nd	4 l.	570

1969 — Five Years

Race	Course	Distance	Ran	Odds	Result	Beaten	Value
Prix de la Seine	Longchamp	1½ m.	8 ran	1–2	WON	2½ l.	2,598
Coronation Cup	Epsom	1½ m.	7 ran	11–4	WON	¾ l.	11,457
Hardwicke Stakes	Ascot	1½ m.	4 ran	11–8	WON	1½ l.	9,257
Eclipse Stakes	Sandown	1¼ m.	7 ran	4–5	2nd	2½ l.	7,605

King George VI & Queen

Elizabeth Stakes	Ascot	1½ m.	9 ran	9–4	WON	2 l.	31,123
Prix Foy	Longchamp	1⅜ m.	8 ran	4–5	WON	2 l.	7,719
Prix de l'Arc de Triomphe	Longchamp	1½ m.	24 ran	4–1	2nd	¾ l.	30,189
Champion Stakes	Newmarket	1¼ m.	9 ran	40–85	2nd	2 l.	7,426

1970 — Six Years

La Coupe	Longchamp	1⅝ m.	4 ran	1–2	WON	½ l.	6,139
Coronation Cup	Epsom	1½ m.	4 ran	4–11	2nd	¾ l.	3,370
Cumberland Lodge Stakes	Ascot	1½ m.	5 ran	4–5	WON	¾ l.	2,999
Prix de Royallieu	Longchamp	1⅝ m.	7 ran	30–100	3rd, d.h.	½ l. 3 l.	482

Ran 24 times, won 13 — £86,470
2nd 6 times, 3rd twice — £50,452

£136,922

Park Top finished second in the Ormonde Stakes to Hopeful Venture, in the Cumberland Lodge Stakes (1968) to Chicago, in the Eclipse Stakes to Wolver Hollow, in the Prix de l'Arc de Triomphe to Levmoss, in the Champion Stakes to Flossy, in the Coronation Cup (1970) to Caliban, and third in the Oxfordshire Stakes to Levmoss and Canterbury.